Grammar
Practice Book

Grade 5

SCHOOL PUBLISHERS

www.harcourtschool.com

ISBN 10   0-15-349912-5
ISBN 13   978-0-15-349912-8

4 5 6 7 8 9 10   073   12 11 10 09

Contents

Contents

Name _____

▶ **Circle each sentence. Underline each fragment.**

1. Juan moved to a new school.

2. The friends played basketball in the yard.

3. took the bus to school.

4. Mrs. Janis, the math teacher.

5. handed out tests.

6. The teacher collected the homework.

▶ **Label each line of words as a *sentence* or a *fragment*. Add words to each fragment to make a complete declarative sentence.**

7. Pedro and Ito traded baseball cards.

   _____

8. walked to school.

   _____

9. Tamara jogged around the block.

   _____

10. The teacher gave the first test on Friday.

    _____

11. girls soccer after school.

    _____

12. Michelle and Denzel exchanged books.

    _____

Try This

Write three declarative sentences about what you did in school today. Then write three interrogative sentences about what a friend did in school today.

Grammar Practice Book
© Harcourt • Grade 5

Name _____

▶ **Write the interrogative sentences correctly, using capital letters and end marks.**

1. what did you eat for lunch

   _____

2. did you pick out a book at the school library

   _____

3. when did you get a new computer

   _____

4. who helped you with the homework

   _____

5. where did the teacher go

   _____

▶ **If the interrogative sentence is correct, write** *correct.* **Rewrite the incorrect sentences correctly.**

6. Why does Neil miss so many rehearsals

   _____

7. How does the librarian organize the books?

   _____

8. Where is the swimming pool

   _____

9. What time is soccer practice?

   _____

10. When do we get our report cards?

   _____

Grammar Practice Book
© Harcourt • Grade 5

▶ **Read this part of a student's rough draft. Then answer the questions below.**

> (1) Peri has been such a wonderful friend? (2) She helped me in so many ways when I broke my arm falling off the parallel bars. (3) while others in the class laughed at my clumsy fall, she ran to my side right away. (4) and went with me to the doctor to have my arm x-rayed? (5) She carried my books to my classes, and she kept me laughing (6) Do you understand why I think she is such a good friend?

1. Which sentence does NOT express a complete thought?
   A Sentence 1
   B Sentence 2
   C Sentence 3
   D Sentence 4

2. Which declarative sentence has an incorrect end mark?
   A Sentence 1
   B Sentence 2
   C Sentence 3
   D Sentence 6

3. Which declarative sentence has an error in capitalization?
   A Sentence 1
   B Sentence 2
   C Sentence 3
   D Sentence 5

4. Which of these is NOT a declarative sentence?
   A Sentence 1
   B Sentence 2
   C Sentence 3
   D Sentence 6

5. Which of these is an interrogative sentence?
   A Sentence 2
   B Sentence 3
   C Sentence 4
   D Sentence 6

6. Which of these sentences has a missing end mark?
   A Sentence 2
   B Sentence 3
   C Sentence 5
   D Sentence 6

Grammar Practice Book
© Harcourt • Grade 5

Name _____

▶ **Circle the interrogative sentences. Underline the declarative sentences.**

1. How does Jay like his new school?

2. What does Karen enjoy most about her school?

3. Sara takes piano lessons.

4. Keisha reads magazines about travel.

5. Jay helps Lisa with the math homework.

6. How does Susan prepare for the physical education test?

▶ **If the sentence is correct, write** *correct*. **Rewrite the incorrect sentences correctly.**

7. What is the name of the coach.

   _____

8. John and Roberto play basketball every Saturday.

   _____

9. what does Lisa discover about her new neighborhood?

   _____

10. Gale tries out for the volleyball team.

    _____

11. Why is Tim waiting to see the teacher.

    _____

12. I will look in my desk for the calculator?

    _____

Grammar Practice Book
© Harcourt • Grade 5

▶ **Circle the imperative sentences. Underline the exclamatory sentences.**

1. Our coach figures out great strategies!

2. Pitch a curve ball.

3. Jill hit the most doubles!

4. Throw the ball to third base.

5. Keep score of the game.

6. We won!

▶ **Rewrite each sentence as an imperative sentence or an exclamatory sentence. Use correct end marks. Label it as *imperative* or *exclamatory*.**

7. Leslie hit a home run

_____

8. Slide into the base before he can tag you

_____

9. Wei made an amazing catch

_____

10. Throw a fastball

_____

11. I can't believe I struck out

_____

12. Walk to first base

_____

 Try This

Write two imperative sentences and two exclamatory sentences about your favorite sport. Label each type of sentence.

Grammar Practice Book
© Harcourt • Grade 5

Name _____

▶ **Write the interjections in the following sentences.**

1. Wow, Randi hit a home run! _____

2. Oops, Jeff hit a foul ball. _____

3. Oh, no, I can't believe he missed that one. _____

4. Hey, Jessie caught that fly ball! _____

5. Oh, I struck out. _____

6. Whoa, Jorge made it to second base just in time! _____

7. Aha, Jamie stole third base! _____

▶ **Rewrite each sentence, adding an interjection. Remember to use correct punctuation.**

8. Jorge bats next.

   _____

9. She tied the game.

   _____

10. Don't hit that pitch.

    _____

11. Shauna made a base hit.

    _____

12. We won the game!

    _____

13. I stubbed my toe.

    _____

14. I am hungry and tired.

    _____

15. Let's go to the snack bar.

    _____

▶ Read this part of a student's rough draft. Then answer the questions below.

> (1) Wow, our basketball team is going to the state finals! (2) Now we need to get ready. (3) Be at practice on time. (4) Work together as a team? (5) Then get out there and play your best. (6) It will be a very exciting game!

1. Which of the following is an exclamatory sentence?
   A Sentence 2
   B Sentence 3
   C Sentence 5
   D Sentence 6

2. Which of the following contains an interjection?
   A Sentence 1
   B Sentence 2
   C Sentence 3
   D Sentence 4

3. Which imperative sentence has an incorrect end mark?
   A Sentence 2
   B Sentence 3
   C Sentence 4
   D Sentence 5

4. Which is NOT an imperative sentence?
   A Sentence 2
   B Sentence 3
   C Sentence 4
   D Sentence 5

5. Which are the imperative sentences?
   A Sentences 1, 2, and 3
   B Sentences 2, 3, and 4
   C Sentences 3, 4, and 5
   D Sentences 4, 5, and 6

6. Which of these is NOT an interjection?
   A Wow!
   B Ah!
   C Alas!
   D This is cool!

Name _____

▶ **Rewrite the following as imperative sentences.**

1. The batter hits the ball into the outfield.

_____

2. The outfielder throws the ball to third base.

_____

3. The hitter bunts the ball.

_____

4. He tags the runner out.

_____

5. She steals a base.

_____

▶ **Label each of the following as an *exclamatory sentence* or an *interjection*. Add a related exclamatory sentence after each interjection.**

6. Oh, no!

_____

7. The mayor came to the game!

_____

8. Wow!

_____

9. We won the championship for the third season in a row!

_____

10. No way!

_____

Grammar Practice Book

Name _____

▶ **Circle the subject. Underline the predicate.**

1. Jo practiced the piano every day.

2. The two violinists played a duet.

3. The orchestra rehearsed in the auditorium.

4. The musicians practiced every day until the concert.

5. Sophie sang in the school chorus.

▶ **Rewrite these sentences, putting the words in an order that makes sense. Circle the subject and underline the predicate.**

6. jazz Allen listened to.

   _____

7. beautiful wrote songs Leslie.

   _____

8. a flute bought Eric.

   _____

9. the violin Michael played.

   _____

10. gathered around everyone the piano.

    _____

11. gave the quartet a concert.

    _____

 Try This

Write three sentences about your favorite music. Circle the subject and underline the predicate in each sentence.

▶ **Label each line of words as a *sentence* or a *fragment*. Add
a subject to each fragment to make a complete sentence,
and write it on the line.**

1. Janet sang at the town hall.

    _____

2. fixed the broken microphone.

    _____

3. found a drum stick on the ground.

    _____

4. bought the concert tickets.

    _____

5. Juan saw a lot of his friends at the concert.

    _____

▶ **Label each line of words as a *sentence* or a *fragment*. Add a predicate to each
fragment to make a complete sentence, and write it on the line.**

6. Alex and Maria.

    _____

7. Matthew

    _____

8. The musicians.

    _____

9. Her father fixed the broken CD player.

    _____

10. Rachel.

    _____

▶ **Read this part of a student's rough draft. Then answer the
questions below.**

> (1) There are some very talented musicians in our school. (2)
> Alisha played violin in a concert at the community center. (3) Nathaniel
> played the cello on national radio. (4) _____ won first prize in a
> piano competition. (5) Sometimes, these musicians _____.

1. Which is the subject of
   Sentence 2?
   A violin
   B Alisha
   C played violin
   D center

2. Which is the predicate of
   Sentence 3?
   A played the cello on
      national radio
   B Nathaniel played
   C Nathaniel
   D on national radio

3. Which of these is missing
   a predicate?
   A Sentence 2
   B Sentence 3
   C Sentence 4
   D Sentence 5

4. Which of these is missing
   a subject?
   A Sentence 2
   B Sentence 3
   C Sentence 4
   D Sentence 5

5. Which should go in the
   blank in Sentence 5?
   A play music together.
   B were Matthew.
   C was Alisha.
   D in our school.

6. Which could go in the
   blank in Sentence 4?
   A Second
   B Kelly
   C The violin
   D Played

▶ **Circle the subject and underline the predicate in each
sentence.**

1. The hurricane did not do much damage to the house.

2. The windows were shattered.

3. My friends helped us.

4. I lost my flute in the storm.

5. Angela rushed to the house.

6. My father fixed the roof.

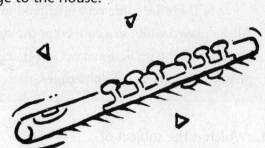

▶ **Write a subject or predicate to complete each sentence. Label the sentence part
that you added.**

7. The school _____

8. _____ were broken.

9. Claire _____

10. _____ raised money
to help homeless people.

11. The orchestra _____

12. _____ donated clothes
and food.

13. Many businesses _____

14. _____ started to
clean up the mess.

15. Her parents _____

Name _____

▶ **Write the complete subject on the line. Underline the simple subject.**

1. The ship sailed from New York City. _____

2. The jazz band planned a tour. _____

3. The empty airplane flew to Italy. _____

4. The crowded bus traveled slowly. _____

5. A long line formed in front of the museum. _____

6. The tour guide showed us the exhibit. _____

7. We wanted to visit the Eiffel Tower. _____

8. My mother loved the food in France. _____

▶ **Write the complete predicate on the line. Underline the simple predicate.**

9. John missed the train. _____

10. The group visited the pyramids. _____

11. We walked through a tunnel. _____

12. I rode a camel. _____

13. My sister swam in the Dead Sea. _____

14. We went to the market in Cairo. _____

15. Our guide told us about the town. _____

Try This

Write a sentence about a place you have visited. Underline the complete subject and circle the complete predicate. Then rewrite the sentence. This time, underline the simple subject and circle the simple predicate.

▶ **Circle the simple subject. Underline the simple predicate.**

1. Steven climbed to the top of the building.

2. Julio watched the changing of the guards.

3. Jason went to the wax museum.

4. Amira studied the map.

5. Many people strolled in the park.

6. Our tour group ate dinner at an Indian restaurant.

7. We packed our bags before breakfast.

▶ **Rewrite these sentences, putting the words in an order that makes sense.
Circle the complete subject. Underline the complete predicate.**

8. the road wound village its the way through

_____

9. contained many the interesting shops things

_____

10. the greeted artist his visitors

_____

11. the photographs sale were for

_____

12. 4:00 P.M. left village we the at

_____

13. arrived Joan at the airport

_____

14. Paris from top viewed of the Eiffel Tower the they

_____

▶ **Read this part of a student's rough draft. Then answer the questions below.**

> (1) My class took a trip to Washington, D.C. (2) We went to the Capitol. (3) The whole class went to the Lincoln Memorial. (4) My teacher arranged a tour of the White House for us. (5) It was very exciting. (6) Learned a lot.

1. Which sentence is missing a subject?

   A Sentence 1

   B Sentence 2

   C Sentence 5

   D Sentence 6

2. Which is the complete subject in Sentence 1?

   A class

   B My class

   C took

   D Washington, D.C.

3. Which is the simple predicate in Sentence 2?

   A We

   B went

   C went to the Capitol

   D to the Capitol

4. Which is the complete predicate in Sentence 5?

   A was very exciting

   B It

   C was

   D exciting

5. Which is the simple predicate in Sentence 4?

   A My teacher

   B teacher

   C arranged

   D arranged a tour of the White House for us

6. Which is the simple subject in Sentence 3?

   A The whole class

   B the Lincoln Memorial

   C went to the Lincoln Memorial

   D class

Grammar Practice Book

▶ **Add a subject or a predicate to complete each sentence. Label the part you added.**

1. Joseph _____.

2. _____ broke down three blocks from the hotel.

3. The airplane _____.

4. _____ were at the theater.

5. The taxi _____.

▶ **Write a sentence using the simple subject and the simple predicate given.**

6. I, lost

_____

7. The alarm clock, was

_____

8. Jessie, telephoned

_____

9. We, walked

_____

10. Talisha, saw

_____

Name _____

Read this part of a student's rough draft. Then answer the questions below.

> (1) Why does our school have a talent show every year. (2) Our students have some very unusual talents. (3) Javier performs some amazing tricks. (4) Rianna trained her dog to balance a ball on its nose! (5) Make sure to go to the talent show. (6) It is a lot of fun and full of surprises!

1. Which is a correct declarative sentence?
   A Sentence 1
   B Sentence 2
   C Sentence 5
   D Sentence 6

2. Which is an imperative sentence?
   A Sentence 2
   B Sentence 3
   C Sentence 4
   D Sentence 5

3. Which sentence has an incorrect end mark?
   A Sentence 1
   B Sentence 2
   C Sentence 3
   D Sentence 5

4. Which type of sentence is Sentence 1?
   A declarative
   B exclamatory
   C interrogative
   D imperative

5. Which is an exclamatory sentence?
   A Sentence 1
   B Sentence 2
   C Sentence 4
   D Sentence 5

6. Which type of sentence is Sentence 6?
   A declarative
   B exclamatory
   C interrogative
   D imperative

▶ **Read this part of a student's rough draft. Then answer the questions that follow.**

> (1) I think that Ashley will be a famous violinist some day. (2) Ashley often plays solos in the school concerts. (3) and wins some big competitions. (4) Her teacher has introduced her to some well-known musicians. (5) Ashley practices at least three hours a day. (6) I don't know how she does it!

1. Which is the simple predicate in Sentence 2?
   A Ashley
   B often
   C plays
   D solos

2. Which is the error in Sentence 3?
   A It lacks a subject.
   B It lacks a predicate.
   C It should be interrogative.
   D It should be imperative.

3. Which is the simple subject in Sentence 4?
   A Her
   B teacher
   C introduced
   D musicians

4. Which is the complete predicate in Sentence 4?
   A Her teacher
   B has introduced
   C has introduced her to some well-known musicians
   D well-known musicians

5. Which is the simple predicate in Sentence 5?
   A Ashley
   B practices at least three hours a day
   C at least three hours a day
   D practices

6. Which is the complete subject in Sentence 2?
   A Ashley
   B plays
   C solos
   D concerts

Name _____

▶ **Combine the pair of sentences into one sentence with a compound subject.**

1. The park opened at 8:00 A.M. The beach opened at 8:00 A.M.

   _____

2. Rebecca went to the picnic. Mark went to the picnic.

   _____

3. Eric swam in the ocean. Gabriel swam in the ocean.

   _____

4. Sometimes, Cheryl taught volleyball. Other times, Daniel taught volleyball.

   _____

5. Mom drove Tim to the beach. Sometimes, Dad drove Tim to the beach.

   _____

▶ **Combine the pair of sentences into one sentence with a compound predicate.**

6. I went swimming. Sometimes, I played volleyball instead.

   _____

7. Jessie built a sand castle at the beach. Jessie dug a tunnel through it.

   _____

8. Kareem sat on a bench. Kareem ate ice cream.

   _____

9. Jenna walked along the beach. Jenna collected shells.

   _____

10. We placed the towels on the sand. We opened the beach umbrella.

    _____

Name _____

▶ In each sentence, underline the compound subject or circle the compound predicate.

1. Victoria drew pictures, sculpted clay, and made mosaics.

2. Jonathan, his brother, and their parents made dinner together.

3. We drove to the mall, went shopping, and ate at a nearby restaurant.

4. Lucy, Molly, and Rachel played in the yard.

5. Nicholas, Paul, and Steve went to the gym.

6. Josh, Stacy, Roger, and Linda worked on the project.

7. Denise swam two laps, ran 50 yards, and jumped hurdles in the race.

8. Chan played field hockey, did his homework, and practiced the clarinet.

▶ Use the compound subjects or compound predicates to write complete sentences.

9. Julio, Mary, and Lisa

_____

10. fed the dog, washed the dishes, and swept the floor.

_____

11. Tamika, her parents, and I

_____

12. played checkers, finished a puzzle, and ate dinner.

_____

13. the snack bar, the restaurant, and the cafe

_____

14. practiced the piano, cleaned her room, and went to bed.

_____

15. Matt, Todd, and Mark

_____

▶ **Read this part of a student's rough draft. Then answer the questions that follow.**

> (1) Juanita and her family celebrated Juanita's birthday with a festive picnic in the park. (2) Juanita's parents cooked her favorite foods for the picnic and brought a piñata to hang from a tree. (3) Juanita's sister brought music. (4) Many friends and family members went to the party. (5) They ate, danced to the music, and rushed to grab all the candy that fell from the broken piñata.

1. Which is the compound subject in Sentence 1?
   A Juanita
   B celebrated
   C festive picnic
   D Juanita and her family

2. Which sentence has a compound subject?
   A Sentence 2
   B Sentence 3
   C Sentence 4
   D Sentence 5

3. Which sentence has a compound predicate?
   A Sentence 1
   B Sentence 2
   C Sentence 3
   D Sentence 4

4. Which is the compound predicate in Sentence 5?
   A They ate, danced, and rushed
   B ate, danced
   C ate, danced to the music, and rushed to grab all the candy that fell from the broken piñata.
   D all the candy that fell from the broken piñata

5. Which is the conjunction that joins the two subjects in Sentence 1?
   A family
   B and
   C her
   D birthday

6. Which is the conjunction that joins the three predicates in Sentence 5?
   A They
   B danced
   C and
   D rushed

Grammar Practice Book
© Harcourt • Grade 5

▶ **Underline the compound subject in the sentence. Circle the conjunction that joins the subjects.**

1. Jan and Kate make a presentation about our favorite things.

2. Soccer and baseball are the two most popular sports.

3. Chicken, hamburgers, and corn on the cob are my three favorite foods.

4. Milk and juice are two drinks Luis likes.

5. Oatmeal and broccoli are the two foods I like the least.

▶ **Write a sentence with a compound predicate that answers the question. Underline the compound predicate. Circle the conjunction that joins the predicates.**

6. What do you do on a rainy Saturday?

_____

7. What are three things that you do after school?

_____

8. What are three things you do with your friends?

_____

9. What do you do at the beach?

_____

10. What are two things you do in the morning before you go to school?

_____

Name _____

▶ **Label the sentence as *simple* or *compound*. Circle the conjunction in each compound sentence.**

1. Everyone was excited, for the circus was coming. _____

2. The acrobats performed on the trampoline. _____

3. One clown juggled balls, and the other performed funny stunts. _____

4. The performer climbed a rope up to the trapeze. _____

5. The acrobats must focus their attention, or they might fall off the wire. _____

6. The clown made a coin disappear, but it was only a trick. _____

▶ **Write an example of the type of sentence named. Use commas correctly.**

7. simple sentence

_____

8. compound sentence

_____

9. simple sentence with a compound subject

_____

10. simple sentence with a compound predicate

_____

11. compound sentence with a compound subject

_____

12. compound sentence with a compound predicate

_____

Try This

Write three sentences about your favorite circus act. Include a simple sentence and a compound sentence.

Grammar Practice Book
© Harcourt • Grade 5

▶ **The sentences are combined incorrectly. Rewrite the combined sentence correctly.**

1. The juggler juggled apples, he also juggled oranges.

   _____

2. The clowns made funny noises the mimes made funny faces.

   _____

3. The magician showed an empty hat then he pulled a colorful scarf from it.

   _____

4. The artist could make a balloon in the shape of a poodle I could choose another animal shape.

   _____

   _____

5. My sister went to a different circus last year she said this one was more fun.

   _____

   _____

▶ **Rewrite the run-on sentence as two separate sentences.**

6. The horses circled the ring then they stopped.

   _____

7. The troupe had fifteen people they included clowns and acrobats.

   _____

8. I wanted my face painted like the clowns' faces now my nose has a big red spot!

   _____

   _____

► Read this part of a student's rough draft. Then answer the questions that follow.

> (1) The circus is coming to town I am so excited! (2) Elizabeth and I already have tickets to it. (3) My favorite part is the trapeze artists' stunts, but I worry that the performers might fall. (4) Elizabeth and I love to watch the magicians, but their tricks are too good for us to figure out! (5) We also enjoy watching the balloon artists and love to have our faces painted.

1. Which is a correct simple sentence?
 A Sentence 1
 B Sentence 2
 C Sentence 3
 D Sentence 4

2. Which is a correct compound sentence?
 A Sentence 1
 B Sentence 2
 C Sentence 4
 D Sentence 5

3. Which is a run-on sentence?
 A Sentence 1
 B Sentence 2
 C Sentence 3
 D Sentence 4

4. Which is a simple sentence with a compound subject?
 A Sentence 1
 B Sentence 2
 C Sentence 3
 D Sentence 4

5. Which is a simple sentence with a compound predicate?
 A Sentence 2
 B Sentence 3
 C Sentence 4
 D Sentence 5

6. Which is a compound sentence that contains a compound subject?
 A Sentence 1
 B Sentence 2
 C Sentence 3
 D Sentence 4

Grammar Practice Book
© Harcourt • Grade 5

► Label the sentence as *simple sentence, simple sentence with compound subject, simple sentence with compound predicate, compound sentence, compound sentence with compound subject,* or *compound sentence with compound predicate.*

1. The clowns make us laugh. _____

2. My favorite performer is not in this show, but I think it will be good anyway.

   _____

3. Noah and I wanted to have our faces painted, but there wasn't enough time before

   the show. _____

4. The clowns and the mimes competed for attention from the audience.

   _____

5. The tigers looked scary, but they obeyed their trainer's commands and behaved very

   well. _____

► Rewrite the sentence correctly. Add a conjunction in the correct place.

6. Alex had better be on time, I will go into the tent without him!

   _____

   _____

7. The balloon artists worked before the show, later, they watched the circus with us.

   _____

   _____

8. We live far from the theater, we arrived on time.

   _____

   _____

9. The jugglers struggled, they had too much to handle.

   _____

   _____

10. My favorite show is the circus, I go every year!

    _____

    _____

Name _____

▶ **Underline the prepositional phrase in the sentence.**
Circle the preposition.

1. The Revolutionary War took place between 1775 and 1783.

2. There were many battles during the Revolutionary War.

3. General Washington moved his troops across the Delaware River.

4. The Americans fought with determination.

5. Their love for their country was deep.

▶ **Underline the prepositional phrase. Write on the line the preposition**
and its object.

6. The soldiers moved toward the front line.

   _____

7. The enemy was waiting by the state border.

   _____

8. We waited until dawn to attack the enemy.

   _____

9. The soldiers stood on a narrow bridge.

   _____

10. The soldiers crossed the river to the peninsula.

   _____

🖊 **Try This**

Write a few sentences about the United States. Include a prepositional phrase in
each sentence. Underline the preposition, and circle the object of the preposition.

Grammar Practice Book
© Harcourt • Grade 5

▶ **Choose the correct preposition from the words in parentheses, and rewrite the sentence.**

1. Washington's troops crossed the Delaware River (in, into) small boats.

   _____

2. The Americans escaped (in, into) Pennsylvania.

   _____

3. Hamilton and Monroe were (among, between) Washington's officers.

   _____

4. The American tactics were not like those (by, of) the British.

   _____

5. The army split (through, into) two groups and caught the British by surprise.

   _____

▶ **Choose the correct preposition to go in the blank in the sentence, and write it on the line.**

across	of	at	from	among	for	on

6. The Mohawks were _____ several tribes that sided with the British.

7. Washington used the tactic _____ surprise.

8. American troops crossed the Delaware _____ December 25th.

9. They rowed the boats _____ the icy river.

10. The general prepared his men _____ the attack.

11. The Americans attacked _____ dawn.

12. The Battle of Trenton lasted for two hours _____ the time it started.

▶ **Read this part of a student's rough draft. Then answer the questions that follow.**

> (1) The general spoke to the soldiers. (2) He spoke about the unique spirit of the Americans. (3) He asked the soldiers to face with determination the difficulties that were to come. (4) The soldiers understood the brutal conditions. (5) They knew that together they would triumph over the enemy.

1. Which is the preposition in Sentence 1?
   A general
   B spoke
   C to
   D soldiers

2. Which is the object of the preposition in Sentence 1?
   A general
   B spoke
   C to
   D soldiers

3. How many prepositional phrases are in Sentence 2?
   A one
   B two
   C three
   D four

4. Which is the prepositional phrase in Sentence 3?
   A He asked
   B the soldiers
   C to face the difficulties
   D with determination

5. Which is the preposition in Sentence 3?
   A soldiers
   B face
   C with
   D determination

6. Which sentence does not contain a prepositional phrase?
   A Sentence 2
   B Sentence 3
   C Sentence 4
   D Sentence 5

▶ **Underline the prepositional phrase. Write on the line the preposition and its object.**

1. They sat under a tree.

    _____

2. They fought the battle in the daylight.

    _____

3. The soldiers were stationed around the enemy.

    _____

4. The general watched the cold, wet soldiers step onto land.

    _____

5. The soldiers rose above the challenges and achieved victory.

    _____

▶ **Rewrite the sentence, adding a preposition to fill in the blank.**

6. They carried guns _____ the river.

    _____

7. They hid _____ the bushes.

    _____

8. The soldiers fought _____ freedom.

    _____

9. Another attack _____ dawn was a surprise.

    _____

10. The soldiers were triumphant _____ the end.

    _____

▶ **Each sentence has one or two clauses. Underline the independent clause. Circle the dependent clause.**

1. The artist assembled the materials for her sculpture.

2. She used the room as a studio because it had so much natural light.

3. The assistant prepared the stone before the artist began to sculpt.

4. The artist completed the work in one week.

5. When the artist completed the work, she invited gallery owners to view it.

6. Two gallery owners bid for the sculpture.

7. Many people admired the sculpture.

▶ **Label the sentence as *simple* or *complex*. For each complex sentence, underline the subordinating conjunctions.**

8. The local artists exhibited their latest work. _____

9. When the lecture ended, the artists answered questions from the audience.

_____

10. A girl in my art class won the contest that the museum sponsored. _____

11. Art students come from near and far, although many can walk to the school from

their homes. _____

12. The teachers come from all over the world, which helps students learn different ideas

about art. _____

13. The students examined the paintings at the exhibition. _____

14. The art was still in the gallery, although the show ended yesterday. _____

15. Because we knew that the exhibition would be crowded, we arrived early.

_____

🖊 **Try This**

Write three complex sentences about art. Use subordinating conjunctions such as *although, because, when,* or *that* to join the parts of each complex sentence. Circle the connecting words.

Name _____

Clauses and
Phrases;
Complex
Sentences
. . . .
Lesson 9

▶ **Rewrite the pair of sentences to form a complex sentence.
Use the subordinating conjunctions in parentheses ( ) to join
the parts of the complex sentence.**

1. There were many difficulties. The art school was finally built. (although)

   _____

2. The building was completed. We held an open house. (when)

   _____

3. This art school is special. Its teachers are so talented. (because)

   _____

4. Juan Pedro is an artist. He founded the school. (who)

   _____

5. The teachers gave classes in art history. The classes helped deepen the students'

   appreciation of art. (which) _____

   _____

▶ **Combine the pair of sentences into a complex sentence, using a subordinating
conjunction and inserting the correct punctuation. Underline the subordinating
conjunctions.**

6. The materials arrived. The artist began his work.

   _____

7. The project was challenging. Many people offered their help. _____

   _____

8. More workers were hired. This made the job go faster.

   _____

9. David won the prize. He entered many contests.

   _____

10. The classes were small. The students learned more.

   _____

▶ Read this part of a student's rough draft. Then answer the
questions that follow.

> (1) The school puts on an art exhibition every year. (2) Because each year's exhibition has a different theme, a new student committee is elected to select art for it. (3) Although there are many entries, only three works of art are selected from each grade. (4) After the committee selects each work, the group determines where the art will be displayed. (5) Sometimes the artists are asked to write something about their work.

1. Which of these contains only an
   independent clause?
   A Sentence 1
   B Sentence 2
   C Sentence 3
   D Sentence 4

2. Which of these is NOT a complex
   sentence?
   A Sentence 2
   B Sentence 3
   C Sentence 4
   D Sentence 5

3. Which is the subordinating
   conjunction in Sentence 2?
   A Because
   B is
   C for
   D student

4. Which is the dependent clause in
   Sentence 3?
   A Although
   B Although there are many entries
   C only three works are selected
   D only three works are selected from
     each grade

5. Which is the independent clause in
   Sentence 4?
   A After the committee selects
     each work
   B the committee selects
   C the group determines
   D the group determines where the
     art will be displayed

6. Which is the subordinating
   conjunction in Sentence 4?
   A After
   B the committee
   C selects
   D each

Name _____

▶ Add an *independent clause* or a *dependent clause* as shown
in the parentheses to complete the sentence. Punctuate
sentences correctly.

1. When the student artist showed his work to the teacher (independent) _____

   _____

2. Justin painted standing up (dependent) _____

   _____

3. Although the class was nearly over (independent) _____

   _____

4. _____ Diane bought some more
   colored pencils. (dependent)

5. Before Tisha started to paint (independent) _____

▶ Rewrite the pair of sentences to form a complex sentence. Use the subordinating
conjunctions in the parentheses to join the parts of the complex sentence.

6. The students sketched pictures. Then they painted the mural. (before)

   _____

7. The students completed the mural. They cleaned up. (after)

   _____

8. Jen finished her drawing. She found a place to display it. (when)

   _____

9. It was getting dark. The studio's lights were turned on. (because) _____

   _____

10. The artist chose bright colors for the painting. The painting showed the countryside
    on a rainy day. (although) _____

    _____

▶ Read this part of a student's rough draft. Then answer the questions that follow.

> (1) My friends and I were part of a live audience for a televised cooking show. (2) We watched the preparation of lentil soup, and we saw what happens behind the scenes, too. (3) The chef chopped onion, sliced celery, and diced carrots. (4) He added the vegetables to an oiled pot. (5) He filled the pot with vegetable stock, added the lentils, and brought the mixture to a boil.

1. Which sentence contains a compound subject?
   A Sentence 1
   B Sentence 3
   C Sentence 4
   D Sentence 5

2. Which is a simple sentence with a compound predicate?
   A Sentence 1
   B Sentence 2
   C Sentence 3
   D Sentence 4

3. Which is the subject of Sentence 1?
   A My friends and I
   B audience
   C I
   D cooking show

4. Which is the predicate in Sentence 4?
   A He
   B added the vegetables to an oiled pot
   C the vegetables to an oiled pot
   D an oiled pot

5. Which is the compound predicate in Sentence 5?
   A He filled
   B filled the pot with vegetable stock
   C filled the pot with vegetable stock, added the lentils, and brought the mixture to a boil
   D the mixture to a boil

6. Which of these is a compound sentence?
   A Sentence 1
   B Sentence 2
   C Sentence 3
   D Sentence 4

Read this part of a student's rough draft. Then answer the questions that follow.

> (1) Our class prepared an international buffet lunch, and it was delicious! (2) Carlos brought tacos, which had meat, beans, corn, and peppers in them. (3) Peter brought pasta because he is Italian. (4) Nicholas brought a Greek pastry called baklava. (5) When I arrived home, I told my mother that I had no room for dinner!

1. Which is NOT a complex sentence?
   A Sentence 2
   B Sentence 3
   C Sentence 4
   D Sentence 5

2. Which is the dependent clause in Sentence 2?
   A Carlos brought tacos
   B meat, beans, corn, and peppers
   C which had meat, beans, corn, and peppers in them
   D tacos, which had meat, beans, corn, and peppers

3. Which is the prepositional phrase in Sentence 2?
   A Carlos
   B brought tacos
   C meat, beans, corn, and peppers
   D in them

4. Which is the prepositional phrase in Sentence 5?
   A When I arrived home
   B I told my mother
   C no room
   D for dinner

5. Which is the subordinating conjunction in Sentence 5?
   A When
   B I
   C arrived
   D home

6. Which is the independent clause in Sentence 3?
   A Peter brought
   B Peter brought pasta
   C because he is Italian
   D because

▶ Underline the common nouns. Circle the proper nouns.

1. The crew maintained the supplies on the ship.

2. Jordan Lineman was the carpenter.

3. Martin raised the sail on the mast every morning.

4. The captain named the ship *World Sailor*.

5. The storm lasted for days.

6. The crew cleaned the deck on Tuesday.

▶ Rewrite the sentences, replacing the underlined words with proper nouns.
Use correct capitalization.

7. The <u>captain</u> made an announcement.

   _____

8. The <u>ship</u> traveled to every continent.

   _____

9. The ship carried cargo to <u>two countries</u>.

   _____

10. The storm moved toward the <u>ocean</u>.

    _____

11. <u>My sister</u> and I played together on the deck.

    _____

12. The crew was excited when the ship docked in <u>a city</u>.

    _____

🌀 **Try This**

Write three sentences about a boat or something else you know about. Include both common and proper nouns.

Grammar Practice Book
© Harcourt • Grade 5

Name _____

▶ **Circle the words that can be abbreviated.**
   Write the abbreviations.

1. 3,000 miles   _____

2. Mister Smith   _____

3. Mistress Kane   _____

4. August 14   _____

5. Doctor Myers   _____

6. September 7   _____

7. Friday   _____

8. Pine Street   _____

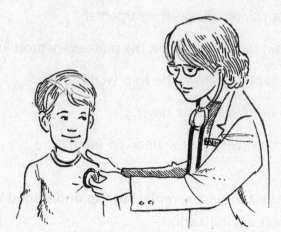

▶ **Rewrite each sentence. Replace each abbreviation with the full word.**

9. Mrs. Redding went back to her cabin.

_____

10. Dr. Selon took care of any sick passengers.

_____

11. We could see Mt. Hood from the ship.

_____

12. Mr. Lotham was a frequent passenger on the ship.

_____

13. The boat entered the St. Lawrence River.

_____

14. The passengers wandered down Charles Ave.

_____

15. Jason Lawson planned to come again in Nov.

_____

Grammar Practice Book
© Harcourt • Grade 5

▶ **Read this part of a student's rough draft. Then answer the questions that follow.**

(1) My favorite activity is boating at camp wilmore. (2) We can go rowing, kayaking, or canoeing. (3) Jessie and Joan, the lifeguards at the camp, took us on a canoe trip in Delaware. (4) The rapids were scary, but we made it! (5) When we returned to camp, Mr. Weston, the head of the camp, was there to congratulate us.

1. Which sentence contains an error in capitalization?
   A Sentence 1
   B Sentence 2
   C Sentence 3
   D Sentence 4

2. How many proper nouns are in Sentence 3?
   A one
   B two
   C three
   D none

3. Which of the following does NOT contain a proper noun?
   A Sentence 1
   B Sentence 2
   C Sentence 3
   D Sentence 5

4. Which is the common noun in Sentence 4?
   A rapids
   B were
   C but
   D made

5. Which sentence contains an abbreviation?
   A Sentence 2
   B Sentence 3
   C Sentence 4
   D Sentence 5

6. Which is the proper noun in Sentence 5?
   A When
   B Mr. Weston
   C camp
   D trip

Name _____

▶ **Underline the common nouns. Circle the proper nouns.**

1. The ship traveled to Alaska.

2. Mr. and Mrs. Pearson were passengers.

3. The crew worked hard to maintain the ship.

4. Spencer and Isabelle played on the deck.

5. Michael went sailing on Lake Garfield.

6. The dishes slid off the tables during the storm.

▶ **Rewrite each sentence with correct capitalization and punctuation. Then underline the proper nouns.**

7. Mr miller greeted the guests on the boat.

_____

8. The boat docked at the marina in monterey, california.

_____

9. We left the port at st augustine, florida, on monday.

_____

10. mrs jenson gazed at the stars.

_____

11. the name of the military ship was the intrepid.

_____

12. my mother and I went rowing on cayuga lake.

_____

Grammar Practice Book

▶ **Circle the singular common nouns. Underline the plural nouns.**

1. Carl is a biologist who studies inhabitants of the sea.

2. A person should be respectful of the habitats of other creatures.

3. One tidal pool can contain many plants and animals.

4. All living things must be able to adapt to a changing environment.

5. Jen read three books this month, but Louis read only one magazine.

6. The counselor lost his watch in a big wave.

7. Andrew complained about his wet sweater and socks.

▶ **Change the nouns in parentheses ( ) from singular to plural and rewrite the sentences.**

8. The red (crab) can be found near the (dock).

_____

9. My (friend) used (worm) as bait.

_____

10. We conducted the (study) at Cobscook Bay.

_____

11. The (boy) ate baked (potato) for lunch.

_____

12. The (seagull) landed near the (bush).

_____

Try This

Make a list of things you can find in your home. Write down and label three items that are singular and three items that are plural.

Name _____

▶ **Rewrite each sentence, using the correct plural form of the noun in parentheses.**

1. We displayed the seashells on the (shelf).

   _____

2. How many (foot) long was the fish you caught?

   _____

3. We ate the fish with forks and (knife).

   _____

4. Sailors lead interesting (life).

   _____

5. Sometimes rats and (mouse) come off the ships, too.

   _____

6. I saw (goose) flying by the shore.

   _____

7. How many (person) visit this beach each year?

   _____

▶ **Write the correct plural form of each singular common noun.**

8. The child loves to swim.   _____

9. The woman goes surfing.   _____

10. The sheep needs to be sheared.   _____

11. I saw a fox.   _____

12. My tooth is hurting.   _____

13. A deer walks into the woods.   _____

14. The thief crept away quietly.   _____

15. The loaf was stale.   _____

Grammar Practice Book
© Harcourt • Grade 5

▶ **Read this part of a student's rough draft. Then answer the questions that follow.**

(1) You may think the desert does not support life of any kind, but that is far from true. (2) A deserts can be home to thousands of different plants. (3) The harsh environment makes survival difficult, but many plant have adapted. (4) Some plants have spiny leaf to slow down evaporation. (5) The cactus is an example of this type of plant. (6) It evolved this way to tolerate extreme heat and endure long droughts.

1. Which sentence has no plurals?
   A Sentence 1
   B Sentence 2
   C Sentence 4
   D Sentence 6

2. Which is the correct plural for *leaf* (Sentence 4)?
   A leafs
   B leaves
   C leafes
   D leafies

3. Which sentence has a plural noun where a singular noun should be?
   A Sentence 1
   B Sentence 2
   C Sentence 3
   D Sentence 5

4. Which sentence has a singular noun where a plural noun should be?
   A Sentence 1
   B Sentence 2
   C Sentence 3
   D Sentence 5

5. Which is the correct plural for *environment* (Sentence 3)?
   A environment
   B environments
   C environmentes
   D environmenties

6. Which is the correct plural for *life* (Sentence 1)?
   A life
   B lifes
   C live
   D lives

Grammar Practice Book
© Harcourt • Grade 5

▶ **Write the singular form of the plural noun in each sentence.**

1. We wore scarves to go out on deck. _____

2. We caught many fish on the last trip. _____

3. The spies hid in the submarine. _____

4. The sailor made knots along the length of the rope. _____

5. My father wore blue ties when he was in the Navy. _____

6. The crab pot had latches on its side. _____

7. The dolphin navigated by listening for echoes. _____

8. Were the knives kept in a safe place? _____

▶ **Replace all singular common nouns with plurals and rewrite the sentences.**

9. The seagull ate Carl's snack!

   _____

10. Be sure to wear rubber boots if you hike through the marsh.

   _____

   _____

11. The bus traveled daily to the harbor in Massachusetts.

   _____

12. He clutched the starfish in his bare hand.

   _____

▶ **Circle the possessive nouns and underline the common nouns that tell what they possess.**

1. Cindy stands on the boardwalk's steps.

2. Greg's boat is docked in New York City.

3. Have you seen the city's marinas?

4. The harbor's shipping office is closed.

5. Peter's friend won the sailing competition.

6. Jan watches the cloud's shape change.

7. The ocean's waves pound the shore.

8. Gusts of wind fill the ship's sail.

9. The girl's hair blows in the wind.

10. Tonya's scarf is in her bag.

▶ **Write the possessive noun in each sentence and label it as singular or plural.**

11. The crew obeyed the captain's orders. _____

12. The ropes' ends were frayed. _____

13. After the storm, the water's surface was still. _____

14. Peter put his duffel bag under the lifeboat's seat. _____

15. Make sure that the cords' knots are tied tightly. _____

16. The crew's bunks were below deck. _____

17. All the cabins' doors were locked. _____

18. The sailors' friends waited for them to come ashore. _____

▶ **Write the correct form of the plural possessive noun in each sentence.**

1. The (womans'/women's) ferry ride lasted thirty minutes.

   _____

2. The ship's cook sharpened the (knives'/knifes') blades.

   _____

3. The captain explained that the cargo was (sheeps'/sheep's) wool.

   _____

4. The (mens'/men's) survival was an extraordinary event.

   _____

5. The (wive's/wives') plan to throw a welcome party was a success.

   _____

▶ **Write each sentence with the plural possessive form of the word in parentheses ( ).**

6. The (child) trip was to a wildlife center near Boston.

   _____

7. In the rodent room, they saw the (mouse) cages.

   _____

8. They visited New England in fall, when the (leaf) colors changed. _____

   _____

9. A program was introduced to help gray (wolf) survival in New England.

   _____

10. Many (people) support helped the program grow.

    _____

▶ **Read this part of a student's rough draft. Then answer the questions that follow.**

> (1) The men's boat is ready to set sail. (2) The men will be away at sea for many days. (3) Their families gather on the dock to wave good-bye. (4) The men kiss their wives and accept their children hugs. (5) One man's family even brings the dog to say good-bye! (6) The captain's son sounds the boat's horn, and the men begin to board.

1. Which of the following has no possessive nouns?
   A Sentence 1
   B Sentence 2
   C Sentence 5
   D Sentence 6

2. How should the underlined word in Sentence 4 be written?
   A childrens'
   B children's
   C childs'
   D childrens's

3. Which is a plural possessive noun?
   A men's
   B families
   C wives
   D man's

4. Which BEST describes the underlined word in Sentence 6?
   A singular noun
   B singular possessive noun
   C plural noun
   D plural possessive noun

5. How many possessive nouns are in Sentence 6?
   A one
   B two
   C three
   D none

6. Which is a singular possessive noun?
   A men's
   B days
   C captain's
   D sounds

▶ **Circle the possessive nouns and label each as *singular* or *plural*.**

1. This country's history is very interesting. _____

2. After many days at sea, the settlers' journey ended. _____

3. The people's supplies did not last the entire winter. _____

4. The first colony's population included many children. _____

5. Up until age eight, boys' clothing was the same as girls' clothing. _____

▶ **Rewrite the sentences. Replace the underlined words with a possessive noun and the word or words that tell what the noun possesses.**

6. The streets of Boston were quiet.

   _____

7. Alisha visited the historical sites of the city.

   _____

8. I read about the lives of women during colonial times.

   _____

9. Rebecca thought the stars and stripes of the flag were a good design.

   _____

   _____

10. He answered the questions the children had about the *Mayflower* voyage.

   _____

   _____

Name _____

► Circle the pronoun and underline the antecedent in
each sentence.

1. Jenna and Ally wanted their science books.

2. The test was difficult, but Denise passed it.

3. Steven studied with Bianca, and she explained the water cycle.

4. Angela said she knew about evaporation and condensation.

5. Jorge studied hard for the test, and he got an A.

6. Before she took the test, Claire was very nervous.

7. Jon let Cesar borrow his notes on precipitation.

8. Jon and Cesar studied until they felt confident.

9. After they took the test, the students had a party.

10. There were 30 students in the class, but only 25 of them went to the party.

► Write the correct pronoun in each blank and label the pronoun as *singular*
or *plural*. If the pronoun is singular, label it as *masculine, feminine,* or *neuter*.

11. Roger announced that _____ wants to build a weather station.

_____

12. Maria would like to help Roger, but _____ schedule is too busy.

_____

13. Evan and Rick watched clouds as part of _____ weather project.

_____

14. Sarah bought several thermometers and put _____ in different places.

_____

15. I checked the weather vane and saw that _____ pointed east.

_____

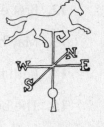

► Write the pronoun and its antecedent in the following
sentences.

1. Joe wanted to be a meteorologist. He kept a weather journal.

   pronoun: _____ antecedent: _____

2. Did you hear the storm last night? It was so loud!

   pronoun: _____ antecedent: _____

3. Ms. Henshaw recorded the temperature. John helped her.

   pronoun: _____ antecedent: _____

4. I had trouble with Mr. Anderson's lesson. Should I ask him for extra help?

   pronoun: _____ antecedent: _____

5. The Davidsons invited Leah to go sledding. They have an extra sled.

   pronoun: _____ antecedent: _____

6. The students saw frost on the ground. It soon melted away.

   pronoun: _____ antecedent: _____

7. I forgot to check the rain guage for Anna. She was not angry.

   pronoun: _____ antecedent: _____

8. Keith and Jenna gave Mia a book about weather. Mia thanked them.

   pronoun: _____ antecedent: _____

► Circle the correct pronoun and underline the antecedent.

9. Brenda went outdoors. Would you like to leave (she/her) a message?

10. My neighbors moved to Alaska. (Their/They) like the snow.

11. At room temperature, ice melts gradually. (It/He) does not melt immediately.

12. Bret explained how water evaporates. (His/He) explanation really helped me!

13. May helped Charlie make a barometer. (It/He) was thankful for the favor.

14. Beth fell on the ice. (Her/Their) arm was sprained, but (him/she) is all right.

15. The boys have left for the lake. If you hurry, you can catch (him/them).

Grammar Practice Book

▶ Read this part of the student's rough draft. Then answer
the questions that follow.

(1) Global warming has become a popular topic among scientists in recent years. (2) Because global warming acts to "put Earth in a greenhouse," it is also called the greenhouse effect. (3) Sunlight enters the atmosphere and then she warms Earth's surface. (4) Pollutants in the air prevent the heat from leaving, trapping the heat in Earth's atmosphere. (5) These pollutants must be controlled because they will cause serious problems if Earth gets too hot.

1. Which sentence uses a pronoun incorrectly?
   A Sentence 2
   B Sentence 3
   C Sentence 4
   D Sentence 5

2. Which pronoun would be an appropriate replacement for the underlined words in Sentence 4?
   A her
   B them
   C it
   D him

3. Which is the antecedent of the pronoun it in Sentence 2?
   A global warming
   B greenhouse
   C effect
   D global

4. Which is the antecedent for they in Sentence 5?
   A global warming
   B Earth's atmosphere
   C the greenhouse effect
   D pollutants

5. Which sentence has no pronoun?
   A Sentence 1
   B Sentence 2
   C Sentence 3
   D Sentence 5

6. Which would be the correct pronoun in Sentence 3?
   A they
   B he
   C it
   D she

Name _____

▶ **Circle the antecedent for each underlined pronoun.
Write whether the word is *singular* or *plural*.**

1. I can't use my bathtub. Water won't go down <u>its</u> drain. _____

2. I telephoned my brothers to ask for help, but <u>they</u> were busy. _____

3. Dinah offered me her tools, but <u>they</u> didn't work. _____

4. The plumber said <u>he</u> can come in the morning. _____

5. Until then, Gina said, I can use the bathtub in <u>her</u> house. _____

6. I asked my landlord if <u>she</u> would pay for the repairs. _____

7. Our lease says that she is responsible. <u>It</u> is in the filing cabinet. _____

▶ **Rewrite the sentences, replacing underlined words with pronouns.**

8. Every winter, my friends call me when <u>my friends</u> know the lake is frozen.

_____

9. Jason said that <u>Jason</u> would go ice-skating, and I want to go with <u>Jason</u>.

_____

10. I am meeting Sarah at the lake. <u>Sarah</u> will help me practice skating.

_____

11. Jenna left <u>Jenna's</u> skates at <u>Jenna's</u> friend's house.

_____

12. Whenever my mother goes ice-skating, <u>my mother</u> has a good time.

_____

Grammar Practice Book
© Harcourt • Grade 5

▶ Read this part of a student's rough draft. Then answer the questions that follow.

> (1) I went traveling with my Family over summer vacation. (2) We drove to canada to see the moose. (3) We stopped at niagara Falls and rode a boat called the Maid of the Mist. (4) The spray from the falls soaked my pants, but my brother theo had an extra pair for me. (5) The souvenirs we bought had maple leaf on them, because there is a maple leaf on Canada's flag.

1. Which sentence incorrectly spells a common noun with a capital letter?
   A Sentence 1
   B Sentence 2
   C Sentence 3
   D Sentence 4

2. Which is the correct spelling of the underlined word in Sentence 2?
   A moosies
   B mice
   C mooses
   D correct as is

3. Which word in Sentence 4 should begin with a capital letter?
   A spray
   B pants
   C theo
   D extra

4. Which is an incorrectly capitalized proper noun in Sentence 3?
   A stopped
   B niagara Falls
   C boat
   D Maid of the Mist

5. Which word in Sentence 2 should be written with a capital letter?
   A drove
   B see
   C canada
   D moose

6. Which is the correct plural of the underlined word in Sentence 5?
   A leafs
   B leafes
   C leaves
   D leavs

Read this part of a student's rough draft. Then answer the questions that follow.

> (1) Jason was a hero in Greek mythology, and he sailed a ship called the Argo. (2) The Argos crew members were known as the Argonauts. (3) The Argonauts had many adventures with Jason. (4) One of the missions of the Argonauts was to sail through the Clashing Islands. (5) These two giant cliffs closed in on anything that traveled between _____. (6) Jason's ship was the first one to pass through the cliffs safely.

1. Which is the antecedent for the pronoun in Sentence 1?
   A Jason
   B Greek mythology
   C ship
   D Argo

2. Which is the correct punctuation for the underlined words in Sentence 2?
   A The Argos crew member's
   B The Argos crew members'
   C The Argo's crew members
   D The Argos' crew members

3. Which pronoun can be used to replace the underlined words in Sentence 3?
   A They
   B It
   C She
   D Its

4. Which is the correct possessive phrase for the underlined words in Sentence 4?
   A mission's Argonauts
   B missions' Argonauts
   C Argonaut's missions
   D Argonauts' missions

5. Which pronoun should go in the blank in Sentence 5?
   A they
   B them
   C her
   D he

6. Which word in Sentence 6 is a possessive noun?
   A Jason's
   B ship
   C one
   D cliffs

▶ **Write the pronoun that could replace the underlined word or words.**

1. <u>Brett</u> writes in his journal every day. _____

2. <u>His new journal</u> is a gift from his older brother. _____

3. Brett says <u>writing</u> is both fun and rewarding. _____

4. <u>Brett's mother</u> encourages Brett to write stories and poems. _____

5. Brett reads three poems aloud to <u>Lee, Clark, and Gary</u>. _____

6. <u>The poems</u> were published in the school newspaper. _____

7. Gary tells <u>Brett</u> that the poems are good. _____

8. The boys ask <u>Brett's mother</u> to join their writing group. _____

9. Then Brett's mother shows <u>her writing prize</u> to the boys. _____

10. <u>The boys</u> are speechless with surprise! _____

▶ **Circle the subjective case pronouns. Underline the objective case pronouns.**

11. I often write newspaper articles with him.

12. Ana gave that assignment to us.

13. She travels to the office with Luis and me.

14. You can ask her for a raise next year.

15. Luis and I have a good time researching stories.

16. It is such an exciting job.

17. We work hard at it all year long!

18. Maybe he will show the photographs to you.

19. They are always interesting.

20. He always knows which picture to give me for a story!

Grammar Practice Book
© Harcourt • Grade 5

▶ Complete each sentence, using either the pronoun *I* or the
pronoun *me*.

1. My friend and ____ wanted to visit the library.

2. My mother drove Nikki and ____ to the bus stop.

3. She gave Nikki and ____ tokens for the bus fare.

4. Nikki and ____ liked the young-adult section best.

5. Next month, Nikki and ____ plan to volunteer at the library.

▶ If the sentence is correct, write *correct*. If it is not, rewrite it correctly.

6. Me and Jennifer read comic books.

_____

7. She and I visited the offices of DC Comics, in New York City.

_____

8. Learning about comics is fun for Jennifer and me.

_____

9. Grandma gave some of her old comics to me and Jennifer.

_____

10. Me and Lisa like to write and illustrate stories.

_____

11. I and Lisa showed her our drawings.

_____

12. Will you buy a comic book made by Lisa and me?

_____

▶ Read this part of a student's rough draft. Then answer the
questions that follow.

> (1) One day, I and my little sister decided to paint some pictures. (2) I found some paper and paints for Missy and me. (3) Missy and I were having fun until she started acting silly by painting her face. (4) I knew that she and me would get into trouble if Mom found a mess. (5) I usually get scolded when there is trouble with me and Missy. (6) I got her to help me clean up the mess, and we were reading a book when Mom got home.

1. In which sentence are the noun and
   pronoun in the wrong order?
   A Sentence 1
   B Sentence 2
   C Sentence 3
   D Sentence 4

2. In which two sentences is the
   pronoun *me* used or placed
   incorrectly?
   A Sentence 2 and 4
   B Sentences 2 and 5
   C Sentences 4 and 5
   D Sentences 4 and 6

3. Which is an objective case pronoun?
   A I (Sentence 1)
   B me (Sentence 2)
   C she (Sentence 4)
   D we (Sentence 6)

4. How should the underlined words
   in Sentence 3 be written?
   A I and Missy
   B Missy and me
   C Me and Missy
   D They are correct.

5. Which is a subjective case pronoun
   that could replace the underlined
   words in Sentence 4?
   A it
   B we
   C they
   D us

6. How should the underlined words
   in Sentence 5 be written?
   A me and her
   B Missy and me
   C Missy and I
   D They are correct.

Name _____

▶ **Fill in the blank in each sentence with a pronoun.**

1. Mom, Dad, and _____ will visit the home of Laura Ingalls Wilder.

2. The museum director has arranged a special tour for Mom, Dad, and _____.

3. "Dad and _____ will pack the car," I said.

4. We are taking some of Wilder's books with _____.

5. _____ plan to have a week of fun.

▶ **Write a sentence using each pronoun below. Then write whether the pronoun is used in the *subjective* or *objective* case.**

6. we

_____

7. it

_____

8. him

_____

9. you

_____

10. me

_____

Grammar Practice Book
© Harcourt • Grade 5

Name _____

▶ **Circle the correct possessive pronoun to complete each sentence.**

1. My cousin likes to tell stories about (her, hers) friends and neighbors.

2. She entertains (our, ours) family with the tales.

3. (My, Mine) town has a storytelling competition each summer.

4. Be sure to practice telling (your, ours) story before the competition.

5. The children tell (their, theirs) stories.

6. Jean's story was the best in (mine, its) category.

7. The grand prize is (her, hers).

8. The Blue Team won (its, theirs) first competition this year.

9. This trophy is (my, mine).

10. (Ours, Its) letters spell the word "Champion."

▶ **Rewrite each sentence. Complete it with a correct possessive pronoun.**

11. Which seats are _____?

_____

12. I think _____ seats are in the fourth row.

_____

13. That seat is _____.

_____

14. The actors exit the stage on _____ right.

_____

15. I can't believe they are performing _____ play!

_____

Name _____

▶ **Circle the reflexive pronoun in each sentence. Underline
the word to which the pronoun refers.**

1. "I will teach myself how to write," said David.

2. David promised himself that he would become a famous writer some day.

3. Kahlen said to David, "We must tell ourselves to stay focused."

4. They worked hard and taught themselves how to write well.

5. You can help yourself by taking a writing class.

6. I took that class and enjoyed myself very much.

7. Rose promised herself that she would sign up for the course.

▶ **Rewrite each sentence. Use a correct reflexive pronoun to replace the underlined
word or words.**

8. Jana and Lori persuaded Jana and Lori to see the play.

   _____

9. Sonja must get Sonja ready, or she will miss her cue.

   _____

10. I will find a ride to the theater for me.

    _____

11. We found us lost in an unfamiliar part of the city.

    _____

12. Mark introduced Mark to the actors.

    _____

60

▶ **Read this part of a student's rough draft. Then answer the questions below.**

> (1) Our small town is peaceful, quiet, and boring. (2) I convinced myself that nothing exciting would ever happen here. (3) One day, my friends and I were enjoying ourselves playing baseball when we heard shouting. (4) People were talking among _____ and pointing at the sky. (5) We arrived in time to watch two men land their hot-air balloon in the town square. (6) The pilot said he had dropped into town to buy _____ a cool drink.

1. Which sentence has a possessive pronoun?
   A Sentence 1
   B Sentence 2
   C Sentence 4
   D Sentence 6

2. Which sentence has a possessive pronoun and a reflexive pronoun?
   A Sentence 1
   B Sentence 3
   C Sentence 4
   D Sentence 6

3. Which is the reflexive pronoun in Sentence 3?
   A my
   B I
   C ourselves
   D we

4. Which reflexive pronoun could fill in the blank in Sentence 4?
   A yourselves
   B itself
   C themselves
   D herself

5. Which is a possessive pronoun?
   A myself (Sentence 2)
   B I (Sentence 3)
   C their (Sentence 5)
   D he (Sentence 6)

6. Which reflexive pronoun could fill in the blank in Sentence 6?
   A itself
   B myself
   C yourselves
   D himself

Name _____

▶ **Circle the correct pronoun in each sentence.**

1. The students will perform a play on (theirs, their) assembly day.

2. Margo has convinced (yourselves, herself) that she should audition for the lead.

3. (Your, Yours) lines are underlined.

4. Please return (my, mine) script after you read it.

5. The scene she is reading is (her, hers) favorite.

6. The stage needs to have (its, their) boards replaced.

7. Chris, you need to read your lines by (yourself, yours).

8. The students asked (themselves, their) if anyone would come.

9. We need to get (us, ourselves) to the auditorium for the play.

10. On opening night, my father drove (ourselves, himself) to the school.

▶ **Use each pronoun correctly in a sentence.**

11. your _____

12. themselves _____

13. yourself _____

14. its _____

15. hers _____

▶ Write whether each underlined adjective is an *article* or
whether it tells *what kind*, *how many*, or *which one*.

1. Laurie's prize calf was kept in <u>the</u> livestock tent. _____

2. She was the <u>first</u> person in her family to win. _____

3. Her mom invited Laurie's <u>two</u> cousins to celebrate with Laurie. _____

4. The <u>red</u> door opened, and someone shouted, "Surprise!" _____

5. Laurie was delighted to see her two <u>Russian</u> cousins! _____

6. Laurie had <u>many</u> things to be happy about today. _____

7. She asked her mom how she kept her cousins' visit <u>a</u> secret. _____

8. "Your <u>helpful</u> friends planned the surprise with me," she said. _____

▶ Write the correct form of the adjective for each sentence.

9. Of all the farm animals, a rabbit is the (fun) to own. _____

10. Of the two rabbits I have, Bouncer is the (playful) one.

    _____

11. She has the (pretty) eyes I have ever seen! _____

12. On the (hot) days of summer, I give her lots of water.

    _____

13. Bouncer hops (fast) than Bertie hops. _____

14. Bouncer is also the (hungry) rabbit. _____

15. The (funny) thing of all is that even my dog Sam likes Bouncer!

    _____

Try This

Write a short paragraph about two pets you know or have read about. Use the
correct forms of adjectives to compare the two pets.

Name _____

▶ **Circle each adjective used to compare. Then underline the basic form of the adjective.**

1. Zach felt that he was a better bass player than singer.

   good   bad

2. His mother said his bass playing sounded worse than a broken record.

   good   bad

3. She thought he was the worst bass player in the world!

   good   bad

4. However, she thought he was the best singer in the whole school.

   good   bad

▶ **Rewrite each sentence, using the correct form of the adjective in parentheses ( ).**

5. Between science and language arts, I am (good) in science.

   _____

6. Among my other four subjects, I am (good) in math.

   _____

7. Of all my classes, I received my (bad) grade in gym.

   _____

8. I have (bad) swimming skills than my friend Karl.

   _____

9. I hope to get (good) grades next year than I did this year.

   _____

10. Ebony has the (good) artistic skills in the whole fifth grade.

    _____

▶ Read this part of a student's rough draft. Then answer the questions below.

> (1) For about two minutes, I thought I was a <u>more better</u> skier than my friend Rose. (2) I was skiing down the <u>most scary</u> bunny slope in the world, and suddenly I was out of control. (3) The <u>taller</u> instructor was yelling at me to sit down. (4) I was the most afraid I had ever been in my life! (5) I skied right through a parking lot and into a flock of Canada geese. (6) It was the <u>worst</u> day of our vacation.

1. How should the underlined words in Sentence 1 be written?
   - A more good
   - B better
   - C most best
   - D Make no change.

2. How should the underlined words in Sentence 2 be written?
   - A more scary
   - B scarier
   - C scariest
   - D Make no change.

3. Which sentence has an adjective that is a correct two-word phrase?
   - A Sentence 1
   - B Sentence 2
   - C Sentence 3
   - D Sentence 4

4. Which describes the word *taller* in Sentence 3?
   - A basic adjective
   - B comparative adjective
   - C superlative adjective
   - D article

5. Which sentence contains an adjective that tells HOW MANY?
   - A Sentence 1
   - B Sentence 2
   - C Sentence 4
   - D Sentence 6

6. Which describes the word *worst* in Sentence 6?
   - A basic adjective
   - B comparative adjective
   - C superlative adjective
   - D article

Name _____

▶ **Rewrite each underlined adjective. Then write whether it is
an *article* or whether it tells *which one*, *what kind*, or *how many*.**

1. The big book fair starts next week at Ring Middle School.

   _____   _____

2. Each student will get one free book with the money raised.

   _____   _____

3. We will donate to the local library all the books that are not sold.

   _____   _____

4. On the third weekend of March, many students will help out.

   _____   _____

5. Few students at the school are not involved.

   _____   _____

▶ **Circle the correct form of the adjective.**

6. You are the (most funniest, funniest) person I know!

7. Of all my friends, you tell the (better, best) jokes.

8. Between you and your sister, you are the (more clever, most clever) comedian.

9. If you have a day that is (worse, worser) than mine, I'll make you laugh, too!

10. Today is the (greater, greatest) day of my life.

11. We told my sister the (more hilarious, most hilarious) joke of all.

12. I have never seen her (happy, happier) than she was today.

Name _____

▶ **Underline the verb in each sentence.**

1. Thomas Edison's mother teaches him at home.

2. He reads many books about inventions.

3. He learns about science.

4. Thomas Edison works in his laboratory.

5. He experiments with telephones.

6. Edison invents many things.

7. A phonograph plays recorded sound.

8. My family plans a trip.

9. We visit the Edison home in New Jersey.

10. Many articles and books praise the inventor.

▶ **Rewrite each sentence, using a main verb to complete each one.**

11. Dee _____ in her garage.

_____

12. She and I _____ the plans for the new toy.

_____

13. Jamie _____ us with the design.

_____

14. Dee's dad _____ to us from the house.

_____

15. The local newspaper _____ us about our invention.

_____

67

▶ **Underline the verb phrase. Then circle the helping verb.**

1. Lisa and Terrence have entered a project in the science fair.

2. Carla has participated this year as well.

3. I could not help her with her project.

4. David should write about the science fair.

5. What did you think about Carla's work?

6. Keira did not enjoy her presentation.

7. The judges will score the projects.

8. Lisa was talking to Terrence about their invention.

9. Lisa is thinking about her next project.

10. Terrence can work on it with her.

▶ **Rewrite each sentence, using a helping verb to complete each one.**

11. Thomas Edison _____ known as an inventor.

_____

12. He _____ created more than one thousand inventions.

_____

13. Shane _____ not convinced that the phonograph is the best invention.

_____

14. I _____ not tell you the subject of my science report.

_____

15. Willa _____ write about Thomas Edison.

_____

▶ **Read this part of a student's rough draft. Then answer the questions below.**

> (1) The young boy _____ risen long before the sun. (2) He _____ not sleep longer. (3) His mind <u>was</u> churning with ideas. (4) He _____ of a new invention. (5) Minutes ago, the boy <u>were sleeping</u> soundly in his bed. (6) But now he _____ on his experiments through the rest of the night.

1. Which helping verb completes the verb phrase in Sentence 1?

   A had

   B have

   C would

   D did

2. Which helping verb completes the verb phrase in Sentence 2?

   A is

   B could

   C have

   D has

3. How should the underlined helping verb in Sentence 3 be written?

   A were

   B did

   C would

   D correct as is

4. Which verb phrase completes Sentence 4?

   A did thought

   B are thinking

   C had thought

   D were thinking

5. How should the underlined verb phrase in Sentence 5 be written?

   A is sleeping

   B was sleeping

   C are sleeping

   D correct as is

6. Which verb phrase best completes Sentence 6?

   A will be working

   B are working

   C were working

   D have worked

Name _____

▶ **Circle the main verb in each sentence. Underline the helping verb or verbs.**

1. None of the players has missed a single class.

2. Derek will probably get the prize for best science project.

3. Ben is winning the Most Improved certificate this year.

4. Our class has placed first in the science trivia competition.

5. The principal will distribute the awards at the school banquet.

6. We would have liked a larger audience for our play about Thomas Edison.

7. Next month the teacher will have auditions for the next play.

8. She would like that as many students as possible take part.

▶ **Fill in the blank to complete each sentence. Include a verb phrase.**

9. The laboratory repairs _____.

10. The inventor _____ for volunteers.

11. Six workers _____ to help with the new work.

12. There _____ many opportunities to share your ideas.

13. I _____ the team for this project.

14. Kara _____ to make her experiment work.

15. Gloria _____ about inventing something also.

▶ **Read this part of a student's rough draft. Then answer the questions that follow.**

> (1) I clean my room each week. (2) Today I ask _____ how I can get the chore done more quickly. (3) I decide to invent a room-cleaning machine! (4) I think that _____ machine will be very successful. (5) I ask my friends if _____ will help me with this plan. (6) We talk among ourselves about how exciting this is!

1. Which pronoun completes Sentence 2?
   A yourselves
   B myself
   C yourself
   D me

2. Which is a subjective case pronoun?
   A I (Sentence 1)
   B the (Sentence 2)
   C my (Sentence 5)
   D ourselves (Sentence 6)

3. Which kind of pronoun is *We* in Sentence 6?
   A subjective
   B objective
   C possessive
   D reflexive

4. Which pronoun completes Sentence 4?
   A him
   B theirs
   C my
   D mine

5. Which pronoun completes Sentence 5?
   A they
   B their
   C themselves
   D your

6. Which kind of pronoun is *ourselves* in Sentence 6?
   A subjective
   B objective
   C possessive
   D reflexive

Read this part of a student's rough draft. Then answer the questions that follow.

(1) Peter pulled the sleeping bag tightly around his shoulders. (2) This was the <u>miserable</u> night of Peter's life. (3) Jeremy and Brad _____ shivering just as he was. (4) The wind was slapping the loose tent flap back and forth. (5) Someone <u>should invent</u> a heated sleeping bag, thought Jeremy. (6) Eventually, the three campers fell asleep, and Peter dreamed that he invented the _____ sleeping bag ever!

1. Which helping verb completes Sentence 3?

   A is

   B was

   C were

   D will

2. Which describes the word *loose* in Sentence 4?

   A It is an adjective.

   B It is a pronoun.

   C It is the main verb.

   D It is a helping verb.

3. How should the underlined adjective in Sentence 2 be written?

   A more miserable

   B most miserable

   C less miserable

   D correct as is

4. Which does the adjective *three* in Sentence 6 tell?

   A which one of the campers

   B what kind of campers

   C how many campers

   D the actions of the campers

5. Which adjective completes Sentence 6?

   A good

   B better

   C most good

   D best

6. Which describes the underlined words in Sentence 5?

   A They make up a verb phrase.

   B They are both main verbs.

   C They are both helping verbs.

   D They are adjectives.

Grammar Practice Book
© Harcourt • Grade 5

Name _____

▶ **Underline each verb. Then identify it as *action* or *linking*.**

1. Ronnie is the best gardener in the neighborhood. _____

2. He comes to the community garden every week. _____

3. After school, Gia rides her bike to the community center. _____

4. She plants flowers by the fence. _____

5. Ronnie and Gia observe their progress. _____

6. When is the open house? _____

7. The garden looks beautiful! _____

8. Ronnie feels tired at the end of a long day. _____

9. Gia makes pizza and salad. _____

10. They eat outside among the plants. _____

▶ **Complete each sentence with the kind of verb shown in parentheses ( ).**

11. We _____ the talent show on Saturday. (action)

12. The teaching staff _____ the contest. (action)

13. I _____ nervous about my performance. (linking)

14. All of my neighbors _____ in the audience! (linking)

15. We _____ a lot of money to give to the school library.
(action)

✎ **Try This**

Write six sentences about your day. Use three linking verbs and three action verbs.

▶ **Rewrite each underlined word and identify it as an** *action*
   verb, **a** *linking verb*, **or a** *direct object*.

1. Carla <u>read</u> a <u>book</u> to learn about sea turtles.

   _____

2. She <u>taught</u> the <u>group</u> about turtles.

   _____

3. The information <u>was</u> very valuable.

   _____

4. The people <u>decided</u> that they would take action.

   _____

5. The community <u>developed</u> a <u>plan</u>.

   _____

6. <u>Write</u> your <u>name</u> on the sign-up sheet if you want to help.

   _____

7. We <u>felt</u> good after our long meeting.

   _____

▶ **Write the verb in each sentence. Then identify the verb as** *action* **or** *linking*.
   Underline the *direct object* **if there is one.**

8. Charles distributes information about the World Wildlife Fund.

   _____

9. He is enthusiastic about their work.

   _____

10. Jan appears interested in the information.

    _____

▶ **Read this part of a student's rough draft. Then answer the
questions below.**

(1) The Garden Club <u>has</u> a <u>meeting</u> every year on May 1st. (2) The members
_____ at Benji's Restaurant to plan the garden. (3) Their garden was once an
abandoned lot. (4) The club has turned the lot into a green oasis. (5) The garden is
a popular meeting place during the growing season. (6) Members share some of the
harvested vegetables and take the rest of them to a local homeless shelter.

1. Which describes the underlined
   words in Sentence 1?
   A linking verb and direct object
   B action verb and direct object
   C linking verb and subject
   D action verb and subject

2. Which is an action verb that could
   complete Sentence 2?
   A meet
   B are
   C become
   D gathers

3. Which sentences have both action
   verbs and direct objects?
   A Sentences 1 and 3
   B Sentences 1 and 4
   C Sentences 3 and 4
   D Sentences 4 and 5

4. Which sentences have
   linking verbs?
   A Sentences 1 and 3
   B Sentences 3 and 4
   C Sentences 3 and 5
   D Sentences 4 and 5

5. Which sentence has two
   action verbs?
   A Sentence 3
   B Sentence 4
   C Sentence 5
   D Sentence 6

6. Which is a linking verb?
   A has (Sentence 1)
   B has turned (Sentence 4)
   C is (Sentence 5)
   D share (Sentence 6)

▶ **Draw one line under each action verb and two lines under
each linking verb. Draw a circle around the direct object
if there is one.**

1. I wrote e-mails to my friend in New England.

2. She became important to me this year.

3. Dora has a house on the ocean.

4. She sent photographs of sea turtles to me.

5. They looked amazing.

6. I am surprised at their size.

7. Sea turtles lay eggs in the sand.

8. The turtles need a safe beach.

9. Are you certain of that?

10. We became interested in conservation.

11. We felt excited.

▶ **Write two sentences that have action verbs and two sentences that
have linking verbs. Underline the verbs and write *action* or *linking* to
describe each one.**

12.  _____

13. _____

14. _____

15. _____

▶ **Write the correct present-tense form of the verb in parentheses ( ).**

1. Marie and Sal (come) to the car wash to help. _____

2. Donna (carry) water and soap over to the car. _____

3. Gordon (place) his sponge in the bucket. _____

4. Wilma (wash) the tires. _____

5. Clare (fill) the bucket with water again. _____

6. The man in the blue car (drive) onto the lot. _____

7. The car's engine (purr) like a kitten. _____

8. He (watch) the kids working. _____

9. More cars (wait) in line. _____

10. The children (make) money for their project. _____

▶ **Rewrite each sentence, correcting each present-tense verb to agree with its subject.**

11. The kids listens to John's ideas for raising money.

_____

12. He want to have a bake sale.

_____

13. Greg and Paul decides they will bake muffins.

_____

14. Tamika greet everyone with a smile.

_____

15. She thank them for giving money to their school.

_____

Grammar Practice Book
© Harcourt • Grade 5

▶ **Rewrite each sentence. Choose the correct verb in parentheses ( ) to complete each one.**

1. Jesse (lies, lays) down to take a nap.

   _____

2. Please (sit, set) in your assigned seat.

   _____

3. (Lie, Lay) the blanket on the bed.

   _____

4. The hot air balloons (rise, raise) into the air.

   _____

5. Please (rise, raise) your hand if you need assistance.

   _____

6. Paul (sits, sets) his books on the floor.

   _____

▶ **Choose a verb from the box to complete each sentence. Use each verb only once. Write it in present tense, and make sure it agrees with the subject.**

lie	lay	sit	set	rise	raise

7. Uncle Greg _____ in the passenger seat of the van.

8. The volunteers _____ the heavy boxes above their heads.

9. My mother is tired and _____ on the sofa.

10. _____ your bags over there.

11. We _____ the baby in the crib.

12. Our kites catch the breeze and _____ up above the trees.

▶ **Read this part of a student's rough draft. Then answer the questions below.**

> (1) Darrell _____ his jacket on the bench. (2) Lisa _____ her tool bag near the door. (3) Fred <u>choose</u> a piece of wood that is on the floor. (4) Connie measure and mark the wood. (5) Then Cole _____ the power saw. (6) They cut wood to build a lemonade stand.

1. Which present-tense verb could complete Sentence 1?
   A lays
   B lay
   C lies
   D lie

2. Which present-tense verb could complete Sentence 2?
   A sits
   B sit
   C sets
   D set

3. Which is the present-tense form of the underlined verb in Sentence 3 that agrees with the subject?
   A chooses
   B chose
   C choose
   D will choose

4. Which is a present-tense verb that could complete Sentence 5?
   A start
   B started
   C starts
   D will start

5. In which sentence is there correct agreement of subject and verb?
   A Sentence 1
   B Sentence 3
   C Sentence 4
   D Sentence 6

6. How should the verbs in Sentence 4 be written?
   A *measures* and *mark*
   B *measure* and *mark*
   C *measure* and *marks*
   D *measures* and *marks*

Grammar Practice Book
© Harcourt • Grade 5

Name _____

▶ **Circle the correct form of the verb in parentheses ( ) to complete each sentence.**

1. The balloons (rise, raise) in the air.

2. The party (celebrate, celebrates) the opening of a new building.

3. Can you (raise, rise) the flag?

4. Our club (present, presents) the money to the director of the hospital.

5. The doctors and hospital staff (sit, set) in the first row.

6. Several kids (lie, lay) on the grass.

7. Other children (play, plays) nearby.

8. The director (thanks, thank) the community for its contribution.

9. I (set, sit) the microphone down on the podium.

10. I (lie, lay) down on the grass, too.

▶ **Rewrite each sentence correctly. Replace the incorrect verbs.**

11. Jeff lays on the sofa and fall asleep.

_____

12. Katie and Jim lie their books on the counter.

_____

13. Paul sits his camera on the shelf.

_____

14. Mia and Kyle watches the sun raising.

_____

15. I cannot rises my sore arm very high.

_____

▶ **Rewrite each sentence. Change the verbs from the present tense to the past tense.**

1. We move from Mexico to California.

   _____

2. I pack my belongings and load them on the train.

   _____

3. There is a whistle, and the train starts moving.

   _____

4. My mother and father seem happy and excited.

   _____

5. My sister sits next to me and rests her head on my shoulder.

   _____

▶ **Write a sentence using each verb in the box. Use each verb in its future tense.**

visit	fly	care	entertain	play	be	drive

6. _____

7. _____

8. _____

9. _____

10. _____

11. _____

12. _____

▶ Fill in the missing form of each verb.

Verb	Present Tense	Past Tense	Future Tense
1. see	see		
2. climb		climbed	
3. appear		appeared	
4. hurry			will hurry
5. trip	trip		

▶ Write a correct form of the given verb to complete each sentence. Then label each verb used as *present tense*, *past tense*, or *future tense*.

6. Hugo's cat _____ away. (run) _____

7. Andrea _____ a picture of the cat on a poster. (paint) _____

8. Thalia _____ a flyer to the post office. (take) _____

9. She _____ it on the community board. (post) _____

10. After school, Hugo _____ for his pet. (look) _____

11. His friends _____ him search. (help) _____

12. Steve _____ his bicycle across town. (ride) _____

13. Duane _____ all the neighbors. (call) _____

14. Marcella _____ the paper for notices. (read) _____

15. Late at night, the phone _____. (ring) _____

16. Mrs. Lopez _____ the call. (answer) _____

17. Gina _____ the cat in the schoolyard. (see) _____

18. The children _____ and shout with joy. (jump) _____

▶ **Read this part of a student's rough draft. Then answer the
questions below.**

> (1) The snow _____ for many hours yesterday. (2) Around
> midnight last night, the wind increase in speed. (3) It howled and shrieked
> outside the house. (4) Earlier this morning, the wind will whip the snow into
> drifts against the walls and doors. (5) My dad will drive us to school in the
> truck today.

1. Which is a past-tense verb that could
   complete Sentence 1?
   A fall
   B falls
   C fell
   D will fall

2. How should the underlined verb in
   Sentence 2 be written?
   A increase
   B increases
   C increased
   D will increase

3. Which sentence correctly uses two
   past-tense verbs?
   A Sentence 1
   B Sentence 3
   C Sentence 4
   D Sentence 5

4. Which sentence correctly uses a verb
   in the future tense?
   A Sentence 2
   B Sentence 3
   C Sentence 4
   D Sentence 5

5. Which sentence incorrectly uses a verb
   in the future tense?
   A Sentence 2
   B Sentence 3
   C Sentence 4
   D Sentence 5

6. Which is the future-tense form of the
   verb *shriek*?
   A shriek
   B shrieks
   C shrieked
   D will shriek

▶ **Rewrite each sentence. Change each verb to its past-tense form.**

1. Jayla will take her kitten to the veterinarian on Saturday.

_____

2. Mr. Vargas smiles at her when she walks past his house.

_____

3. The doctor weighs the cat and checks her for fleas.

_____

4. She announces that the cat's health is excellent.

_____

5. Jayla will give the kitten a treat after the examination.

_____

▶ **Underline the verb in each sentence. Then label each verb as *present tense*, *past tense*, or *future tense*.**

6. Molly lives in the city of Los Angeles. _____

7. Molly and Kim planned a day trip to a hiking trail. _____

8. They will ask Milo, too. _____

9. He will arrive after lunch. _____

10. The trail needs better markers. _____

11. The heat made them tired. _____

12. They lose interest in the hiking trail. _____

13. The friends will ride bikes to the beach instead. _____

14. Molly, Kim, and Milo swim in the cool ocean water. _____

Name _____

▶ Underline each verb phrase. Circle the main verb. Then label each verb as *present perfect* or *past perfect*.

1. The entire student body has assembled in the auditorium. _____

2. Mrs. Smith had purchased a flower for each of her children. _____

3. Kristen had never seen so many colorful flowers. _____

4. The students have visited every house on the street. _____

5. They have collected 300 cans of food for the shelter. _____

6. The students had exceeded their goal. _____

▶ Write a sentence using each verb in the tense shown in parentheses ( ).

7. keep (present perfect)

_____

8. escape (past perfect)

_____

9. leave (past perfect)

_____

10. fly (past perfect)

_____

11. lay (present perfect)

_____

12. observe (past perfect)

_____

▶ **Write the future-perfect form of each verb.**

1. learn   _____

2. speak   _____

3. write   _____

4. sell   _____

5. lift   _____

6. be   _____

7. tell   _____

8. pour   _____

▶ **Write sentences using the future-perfect tense of the verbs below. Use each verb only once.**

finish   build   read   grow

9. _____

10. _____

11. _____

12. _____

▶ **Read this part of a student's rough draft. Then answer the questions below.**

(1) Lucas has wanted to ride the Super Coaster for as long as he can remember. (2) He will have <u>achieve</u> his goal after today's trip to Mega Park. (3) "The day has finally arrived!" he thought. (4) He had dreamed of riding on Super Coaster many times. (5) Finally, Lucas approaches the ride with a mixture of fear and excitement. (6) In a matter of minutes, he will have taken the ride of his lifetime.

1. Which is the verb phrase in Sentence 1?
   A has
   B wanted to ride
   C has wanted
   D to ride

2. Which verb form should replace the underlined word in Sentence 2?
   A achieves
   B achieving
   C achieved
   D to achieve

3. Which form of the verb *dream* is used in Sentence 4?
   A past-perfect tense
   B future-perfect tense
   C present-perfect tense
   D past tense

4. Which sentence correctly uses a verb in the present tense?
   A Sentence 3
   B Sentence 4
   C Sentence 5
   D Sentence 6

5. Which form of the verb *arrive* is used in Sentence 3?
   A present-perfect tense
   B past-perfect tense
   C future-perfect tense
   D present tense

6. Which form of the verb *take* is used in Sentence 6?
   A past-perfect tense
   B future-perfect tense
   C present-perfect tense
   D past tense

▶ **Underline the verb phrase in each sentence. Then identify the tense of each one as *present perfect*, *past perfect*, or *future perfect*.**

1. The class has gone on a field trip to the science museum. _____

2. When they return, they will have learned about city habitats.

   _____

3. Jenny had decided to write her science paper on birds that live in cities.

   _____

4. The library will have closed long before she arrives.

   _____

5. Who has borrowed my science book? _____

6. Yvonne had said Jenny could use her book. _____

▶ **Write a sentence using each verb. Use the verb tense shown in parentheses ( ).**

7. draw (present perfect)

   _____

8. choose (past perfect)

   _____

9. paint (future perfect)

   _____

10. help (present perfect)

   _____

11. make (past perfect)

   _____

12. improve (present perfect)

   _____

   _____

▶ **Read this part of a student's rough draft. Then answer the questions below.**

(1) It is the day of the big charity soccer match, and Jenna feel nervous. (2) She _____ on her bed and pulls on her new soccer shoes. (3) Jenna's mom is excited as she starts the car and drives Jenna to the match. (4) Jenna play her best soccer ever during today's match! (5) All of her friends cheers her on. (6) After the match, she _____ the trophy high above her head!

1. Which sentence has an action verb that does NOT agree with its singular subject?
   A Sentence 1
   B Sentence 3
   C Sentence 4
   D Sentence 5

2. Which is a linking verb in Sentence 3?
   A is
   B as
   C starts
   D drives

3. Which verb could complete Sentence 2?
   A sets
   B set
   C sits
   D sit

4. Which sentence has an action verb that does NOT agree with its plural subject?
   A Sentence 1
   B Sentence 3
   C Sentence 4
   D Sentence 5

5. Which verb could complete Sentence 6?
   A raises
   B raise
   C rises
   D rise

6. Which sentence has a linking verb that does NOT agree with its subject?
   A Sentence 1
   B Sentence 3
   C Sentence 4
   D Sentence 5

Grammar Practice Book
© Harcourt • Grade 5

▶ **Read this part of a student's rough draft. Then answer the questions below.**

> (1) Ms. Luiz will have given the order to start digging. (2) She had asked everyone to join in the hard work. (3) "I told the mayor that we had completed this garden by 5:00 P.M. today!" said Ms. Luiz. (4) "Julio, what had you done with your shovel?" she asked. (5) After many hours, the crew of workers finished all of the planting and watering. (6) By the time she leaves, Ms. Luiz will have thanked every volunteer.

1. Which verb form should replace the underlined words in Sentence 1?
   A have given
   B had given
   C giving
   D give

2. Which form of the verb *ask* is used in Sentence 2?
   A past-perfect tense
   B present-perfect tense
   C present tense
   D future tense

3. In Sentence 3, how could the verb *complete* be changed to future-perfect tense?
   A complete
   B will have completed
   C had completed
   D have completed

4. Which verb form should replace the underlined words in Sentence 4?
   A have done
   B were done
   C are done
   D correct as is

5. Which sentence correctly uses a verb in the past tense?
   A Sentence 1
   B Sentence 3
   C Sentence 5
   D Sentence 6

6. Which is the verb tense of the underlined verb phrase in Sentence 6?
   A present-perfect tense
   B future-perfect tense
   C past-perfect tense
   D future tense

Name _____

▶ **Rewrite each sentence with the past-tense form of the verb in parentheses ( ).**

1. Lewis and Clark (begin) their journey.

   _____

2. The party of explorers (go) very far.

   _____

3. They (find) a route to the west coast.

   _____

4. The Native Americans (speak) to the explorers.

   _____

5. Lewis and Clark (keep) a journal of their travels.

   _____

6. They (spend) time making maps, too.

   _____

▶ **Use the past-tense form of a word in the box to complete each sentence.**

| swim | come | know | run |

7. Lewis and Clark _____ they had a long way to go.

8. The explorers _____ along the riverbank.

9. The horses _____ across the river to the other side.

10. Eventually, the expedition _____ to an end.

✏ **Try This**

Write sentences, using the past-tense forms of these irregular verbs: *lie, lay, sit,* and *fly.*

Grammar Practice Book
© Harcourt • Grade 5

▶ **1.–10. Complete the chart with the principal parts of each verb.**

Infinitive	Present Participle	Past Tense	Past Participle
to throw	(is, was) throwing	_____	(have, has, had) thrown
to bring	(is, was) _____	brought	(have, has, had) _____
to eat	(is, was) eating	_____	(have, has, had) _____
to shake	(is, was) _____	shook	(have, has, had) shaken
to take	(is, was) _____	_____	(have, has, had) taken
to forget	(is, was) forgetting	_____	(have, has, had) _____

▶ **Complete each sentence, using the verb and verb form shown in parentheses ( ).**

11. (*buy*, past tense)

President Jefferson _____ territory from France.

12. (*want*, past participle)

He _____ to have the area explored.

13. (*give*, past tense)

He _____ the job to Lewis and Clark.

14. (*tell*, past participle)

Jefferson _____ them to find a route
through the Rocky Mountains.

15. (*study*, present participle)

The men _____ the wildlife.

16. (*make*, past tense)

They _____ a map of the Missouri River.

17. (*buy*, past participle)

They _____ four canoes from Native Americans.

18. (*flow*, present participle)

The water of the river _____ north.

Grammar Practice Book
© Harcourt • Grade 5

▶ Read this part of a student's rough draft. Then answer the
questions below.

> (1) The sun <u>shine</u> and warmed the sand but not the chilly ocean. (2) No one _____ in the cold water. (3) Some of the explorers built a fire. (4) Farther down the beach, a group of officers investigated a small cove they _____. (5) The sun was setting when they left the beach to make camp. (6) A few seagulls _____ in circles above them.

1. Which verb form should replace the underlined word in Sentence 1?
   A shines
   B shining
   C shone
   D shoned

2. Which word could complete Sentence 2?
   A swam
   B swum
   C swimmed
   D swim

3. Which verb form is used in Sentence 3?
   A infinitive
   B present participle
   C past tense
   D past participle

4. Which word or words could complete Sentence 4?
   A finds
   B finding
   C had found
   D founded

5. Which verb form is underlined in Sentence 5?
   A infinitive
   B present participle
   C past tense
   D past participle

6. Which word or words could complete Sentence 6?
   A flies
   B flown
   C is flying
   D flew

▶ Complete each sentence with a verb form from the box.
Then label each verb form as *present participle, past tense,* or
past participle.

| blew   rode   saw   were biting   had ridden |

1. When traveling over land, the men _____ on ponies.

   _____

2. Lewis _____ many miles. _____

3. The explorers _____ storm clouds gathering.

   _____

4. The wind _____ most of the clouds away.

   _____

5. However, insects _____ them all night.

   _____

▶ Complete each sentence, using the verb and the verb form shown in parentheses ( ).

6. (*rest,* present participle)

   The group _____ after a long day of walking.

7. (*drink,* past participle)

   Someone _____ the last of the water.

8. (*hear,* past)

   The men _____ the sound of running water.

9. (*run,* present participle)

   Someone _____ ahead to find the source.

10. (*come,* past participle)

    At last, they _____ to the Columbia River!

▶ **Write the contraction for each underlined pair of words.**

1. <u>I am</u> hoping to find gold. _____

2. <u>It will</u> be a difficult journey. _____

3. <u>They are</u> strong and brave. _____

4. <u>We have</u> got to climb 1,000 feet. _____

5. <u>It is</u> too steep for animals to go up. _____

6. <u>We are</u> carrying our supplies ourselves. _____

7. He said that <u>he had</u> never been so far from home. _____

8. Two men say that <u>they have</u> already had some luck. _____

9. Is this what <u>you are</u> looking for? _____

10. <u>She is</u> holding a nugget of gold! _____

▶ **Circle the word that correctly completes each sentence.**

11. (It's, Its) very cold in the Yukon.

12. (They're, Their) such hardworking miners.

13. They wear (they're, their) boots and helmets.

14. (Your, You're) expected to carry supplies.

15. He carries the bag by (it's, its) handle.

16. "(Your, You're) claim is excellent!" said the man.

17. (Its, It's) located down the road about a mile.

18. (They're, Their) going to be rich!

Name _____

▶ **Write the contraction for each of the underlined words.**

1. Women <u>were not</u> allowed to register a claim for gold. _____

2. The prospectors <u>have not</u> found the town. _____

3. The man said that he <u>does not</u> want to mine at that creek. _____

4. She <u>is not</u> looking forward to the winter. _____

5. The people <u>did not</u> have enough food last year. _____

6. I <u>do not</u> see my supplies. _____

7. <u>Is</u> that <u>not</u> your pack of food? _____

8. We <u>will not</u> be part of that group of prospectors. _____

9. They <u>could not</u> find their way, and they got lost. _____

10. You <u>should not</u> listen to what they say. _____

11. <u>Do</u> you <u>not</u> see how much confusion you caused? _____

12. I'm sorry, but I <u>was not</u> sure of the directions. _____

13. They <u>would not</u> take responsibility for the mistake. _____

▶ **Rewrite each sentence with the correct contraction.**

14. The woman could not believe what she saw.

_____

15. I will not tell anyone about your discovery.

_____

16. She did not say anything to her friend.

_____

Grammar Practice Book
© Harcourt • Grade 5

▶ **Read this part of a student's rough draft. Then answer the questions below.**

> (1) Today, we are going for a ride over the canyon in a helicopter. (2) I hope _____ going to enjoy it. (3) The last tour group said this was _____ favorite day trip. (4) You will have one hour to explore the canyon. (5) You shouldn't wander too far from the landing area. (6) _____ return flight leaves at six o'clock.

1. Which word could replace the underlined words in Sentence 1?
   A we've
   B were
   C we're
   D we'd

2. Which word could complete Sentence 2?
   A your
   B you're
   C you've
   D youre

3. Which word could complete Sentence 3?
   A their
   B they're
   C theirs
   D there

4. Which is the correct way to write the underlined words in Sentence 4 with a contraction?
   A You've
   B You'll have
   C You will've
   D You've had

5. The underlined word in Sentence 5 is a contraction of which words?
   A should have
   B should not
   C should be
   D should are

6. Which word could complete Sentence 6?
   A You'll
   B Your
   C You're
   D Yours

Name _____

▶ **Write the contraction for the underlined words in each sentence.**

1. <u>She is</u> a daring explorer. _____

2. <u>They are</u> thinking about returning to California. _____

3. <u>They are not</u> finding gold here anymore. _____

4. <u>We are</u> out of food. _____

5. <u>You have</u> got two days to make a decision. _____

6. She <u>could not</u> make up her mind. _____

7. <u>I have not</u> had time to decide. _____

8. "<u>I am</u> too tired to plan anything," said the woman. _____

9. "<u>It is</u> time to stop dreaming and go home," he said. _____

10. It <u>should not</u> take very long to pack. _____

11. You <u>will not</u> have to travel so far this time. _____

12. <u>He has</u> found a new trail. _____

13. They still <u>had not</u> decided on a plan. _____

▶ **Underline the word that correctly completes each sentence.**

14. (Its, It's) cold and windy today.

15. (Their, They're) leaving in an hour.

16. (Your, You're) horses are prepared for travel.

17. (Their, They're) saddles are clean and ready.

18. (Your, You're) going to be late.

Grammar Practice Book
© Harcourt • Grade 5

Name _____

▶ **Underline each adverb. Identify whether the adverb tells**
   how, when, where, **or** *to what extent.*

1. The team is climbing carefully. _____

2. They frequently stop to rest. _____

3. A guide often checks the sky for storms. _____

4. Suddenly, the guide waves his arms. _____

5. Everyone looks up. _____

6. The clouds above darken. _____

7. The climbers have to return immediately. _____

8. The team sadly looks at the mountain's peak. _____

9. Then they quickly begin descending the trail. _____

10. They will finish the climb later. _____

▶ **Complete each sentence by using the correct comparative form of the adverb in**
   parentheses ( ).

11. Jason hikes _____ than Tom. (fast)

12. Of all the hikers, Leah walks the _____. (far)

13. I walk more _____ than my sister. (slow)

14. This year's trail map is _____ than last year's map. (good)

15. Mrs. Ruiz speaks the _____ of all the climbers. (soft)

Grammar Practice Book
© Harcourt • Grade 5

Name _____

▶ **Underline the word in parentheses ( ) that correctly completes each sentence.**

1. Jean didn't have (no, any) cooking equipment.

2. Josh couldn't find his backpack (nowhere, anywhere).

3. You shouldn't (ever, never) go camping unprepared.

4. My hiking boots aren't (nowhere, anywhere) to be found.

5. Don't say (nothing, anything) about the missing flashlight.

▶ **If the sentence is correct, write *correct*. If it is incorrect, rewrite it correctly.**

6. John wasn't never afraid of water.

_____

7. Kay has not learned nothing about first aid.

_____

8. Jessie wouldn't never forget her wet suit.

_____

9. My sister has never gone diving with us.

_____

10. Don't say nothing about diving with sharks.

_____

11. Nobody knows more scuba diving facts than Mr. Cain.

_____

12. Liam doesn't need no help packing his gear.

_____

Grammar Practice Book
© Harcourt • Grade 5

▶ **Read this part of a student's rough draft. Then answer the
questions below.**

> (1) Follow the tips, and you will soon know how to pack a backpack properly.
> (2) First, make a list of equipment needed for your trip. (3) Roll your sleeping bag
> tightly, and push it gently but firmly into its stuff sack. (4) Then, _____
> place heavier items in your pack. (5) Pack sunscreen and snacks so that they are easily
> reached. (6) <u>Don't never</u> forget to review your checklist before you leave home!

1. Which describes the adverbs in
   Sentence 1?
   A *Soon* tells where; *properly* tells
      how.
   B *Soon* tells when; *properly* tells
      when.
   C *Soon* tells when; *properly* tells how.
   D *Soon* tells to what extent; *properly*
      tells when.

2. Which word in Sentence 2 is an
   adverb?
   A First
   B of
   C for
   D trip

3. Which is NOT an adverb in
   Sentence 3?
   A tightly
   B push
   C gently
   D firmly

4. Which is an adverb that could
   complete Sentence 4?
   A not
   B fast
   C slower
   D carefully

5. Which word in Sentence 5 is an
   adverb?
   A and
   B that
   C so
   D easily

6. Which words should replace the
   underlined words in Sentence 6?
   A Don't ever
   B Do not never
   C In no way
   D Do ever

▶ **Underline the word or words that correctly complete each sentence.**

1. The group sits (quiet, quietly) in the plane.

2. Daeshaun prepares (more eagerly, most eagerly) than Tom.

3. This jump is (easy, easily) for him.

4. Corrine (slowly, slow) fastens her belt.

5. Hal puts on his parachute (fast, faster) than Sue.

6. He (soon, soonest) gets ready.

7. I fly a plane (well, better) than my sister.

8. Rae skydives (well, better).

▶ **If the sentence is correct, write *correct*. If it is incorrect, rewrite it correctly.**

9. I don't know nothing about trapeze artists.

_____

10. He hasn't never seen the circus.

_____

11. Marcy does not have no time to learn the routine.

_____

12. She has not had none all week.

_____

13. I would do anything to fly high like that!

_____

14. They don't never manage to finish the show on time.

_____

Grammar Practice Book
© Harcourt • Grade 5

▶ **1.–10. Circle ten words that should be capitalized in the letter.**

1317 Park street
Orlando, FL 32801
june 11, 2008

carsons, Incorporated
708 third Avenue
Houston, TX 77069

dear sir or madam:
I am returning the DVD you sent to me.
It arrived damaged and cannot be used.
please refund my money.

sincerely,
carolina Ruiz

▶ **Rewrite each sentence with the correct capitalization and punctuation. Underline words that should be *italic*.**

11. My report is called a walk on the moon.

_____

12. My mother reads the magazine newsweek.

_____

13. Did you see the movie apollo 13?

_____

14. Let's sing the song rocket man.

_____

15. The last chapter in the book was called space travel in the future.

_____

▶ **Read each sentence. Add quotation marks where they are needed.**

1. What should we do about our science project? Mark asked.

2. Dan said, I think we should make a model of an early spacecraft.

3. That's a good idea, replied Egan. Let's make a plan.

4. I will do the research, said Ben, if Dan and Mark gather the materials.

5. I agree, Ben, Mark said. I'd be glad to work with Dan.

6. We can meet at my house and get started, suggested Egan.

7. I'll bring some of my mom's brownies, offered Dan, if you'd like me to.

8. I'm allergic to chocolate, whined Egan.

9. That's no problem, said Dan. I'll bring some fig bars, too.

10. Let's do it, they said.

▶ **Rewrite each sentence. Use correct punctuation, quotation marks, and capital letters.**

11. where are you studying today dad asked.

_____

12. let's call Rosa suggested Becky.

_____

13. yes, give her a call said Sue and ask her to meet us.

_____

14. i will meet you there said rosa

_____

▶ **Read this part of a student's rough draft. Then answer the questions below.**

(1) Let me read you the note I wrote to Aunt Kathy, said Josh. (2) "I want to thank her for sending the book the coming of space travel. (3) dear aunt kathy, (4) thank you for the copy of the coming of space travel. (5) My favorite chapter so far is called walking on the moon. (6) your nephew, josh."

1. Which punctuation is needed in Sentence 1?

　A quotation marks before *Let* and after *Josh*

　B a comma after *wrote*

　C quotation marks before *Let* and after *Kathy,*

　D a comma after *you*

2. Which is the correct way to show the title of the book in Sentence 2?

　A *The Coming of Space Travel*

　B The Coming Of Space Travel

　C "The Coming Of Space Travel"

　D "the coming of space travel"

3. Which is the correct way to write the greeting of Josh's letter in Sentence 3?

　A Dear aunt kathy,

　B Dear Aunt Kathy,

　C Dear aunt Kathy,

　D dear aunt Kathy

4. Which words in Sentence 4 should start with capital letters?

　A Thank, Coming, Space, Travel

　B Thank, Coming, Of, Space, Travel

　C Thank, Space, Travel

　D Thank, The, Coming, Space, Travel

5. How should the chapter title in Sentence 5 be written?

　A "Walking on the Moon."

　B "Walking on the moon."

　C *walking on the moon.*

　D *"Walking on the Moon."*

6. Which is the correct way to write Sentence 6?

　A Your Nephew, Josh

　B Your nephew, Josh

　C your nephew, Josh

　D Your nephew Josh

▶ **Rewrite the parts of a letter. Use capital letters and correct punctuation.**

1. dear monty _____

2. your friend _____

3. dear sir or madam _____

4. sincerely yours _____

5. write soon _____

6. dear mrs barnes _____

7. yours truly _____

8. 847 north waterview drive _____

9. chicago il 60613 _____

10. april 17, 2008 _____

▶ **Rewrite each sentence. Use correct punctuation. Underline words that should be *italic*.**

11. maybe we can write a report about neil armstrong suggested anne

_____

12. that's a good idea said diane let's get started

_____

13. Mai read the chapter laika to her sister

_____

14. our universe is a popular book

_____

▶ Read this part of a student's rough draft. Then answer the questions below.

> (1) My friend Ava has lived on Florida's Gulf Coast for two years.
> (2) _____ really fun to visit her. (3) We are both serious bird-watchers.
> (4) We like to use binoculars to watch the birds fly around and build _____
> nests. (5) The birds haven't never disappointed us. (6) We are thinking about taking
> photographs of them next time!

1. Which names the form of the verb *live* used in Sentence 1?
   A past participle
   B present participle
   C past tense
   D infinitive

2. Which word could complete Sentence 2?
   A It'd
   B It'll
   C It's
   D Its

3. Which contraction could replace the underlined words in Sentence 3?
   A We'll
   B We're
   C We've
   D We'd

4. Which pronoun best completes Sentence 4?
   A their
   B they're
   C it's
   D its

5. How should the underlined words in Sentence 5 be written?
   A haven't ever
   B have not never
   C hadn't never
   D have'nt ever

6. Which names the form of the verb *think* used in Sentence 6?
   A past tense
   B past participle
   C present participle
   D infinitive

Read this part of a student's rough draft. Then answer the questions below.

(1) Can Neil be persuaded to help us with the play? asked Marla. (2) "If you ask me," said Keisha, "I think Neil will be the easy convinced of all." (3) "Let's find a way to get more students to join the drama club," said Mandy enthusiastically. (4) "I'll ask Mr. Jennings to speak to the class" suggested Kate. (5) "I don't think the students have read macbeth," said Mr. Jennings. (6) "i think the show will go on!" exclaimed Marla.

1. Where should quotation marks be inserted in Sentence 1?
   A after *play?*
   B before *help* and after *play?*
   C before *Can*
   D before *Can* and after *play?*

2. Which form of the underlined adverb in Sentence 2 should be used?
   A most easily
   B more easily
   C easier
   D easiest

3. Which word in Sentence 3 is described by the adverb *enthusiastically?*
   A find
   B get
   C join
   D said

4. Which is missing from Sentence 4?
   A period
   B quotation marks
   C comma
   D capitalization

5. Which is the correct way to write the underlined title of the play in Sentence 5?
   A "macbeth"
   B "Macbeth"
   C *Macbeth*
   D *"Macbeth"*

6. Which is wrong in Sentence 6?
   A period
   B quotation marks
   C comma
   D capitalization

INDEX

A

Abbreviations, 38–39
Action verbs, 73–76, 89
Adjectives
articles, 63, 66
comparing with, 63–66, 72
Adverbs, 99–102, 108
comparing with, 99, 100, 102, 108
Antecedents
agreement with pronouns, 49–52, 54
Apostrophes
in contractions, 95–98, 107
in possessive nouns, 45–48, 54

C

Capitalization, 103–106
letters, 103, 105–106
proper nouns, 37, 39–40, 53, 103
quotations, 104, 106, 108
sentences, 2–3
titles, 103, 105–106, 108
Clauses
dependent, 31, 33–34, 36
independent, 31, 33–34, 36
Commas
complex sentences, 32, 34
compound sentences, 23–24
compound subjects and predicates,
19–22
letters, 102, 106
quotations, 104, 106, 108
Common nouns, 37, 39–42, 44, 53
Complete predicates, 13–16, 18
Complete sentences, 1, 3, 10

Complete subjects, 13–16, 18
Complex sentences, 31–34, 36
Compound predicates, 19–22, 25–26, 35
Compound sentences, 23–26, 35
Compound subjects, 19–22, 25–26, 35
Conjunctions, 19–24, 26
subordinating, 31–34, 36
Contractions, 95–98, 107

D

Declarative sentences, 1–4, 17
Dependent clauses, 31, 33–34, 36
Direct objects, 74–76

E

End marks, 2–3, 5–7, 17
Exclamatory sentences, 5–8, 17

F

Feminine pronouns, 49
Fragments, sentence, 1, 3, 10
Future-perfect verbs, 86–88, 90
Future-tense verbs, 81–84, 90

H

Helping verbs, 68–70, 72

I

Imperative sentences, 5–8, 17
Independent clauses, 31, 33–34, 36
Infinitives, 92–93, 107
Interjections, 6–8
Interrogative sentences, 1–4, 17

INDEX

Grammar Practice Book
© Harcourt • Grade 5